Our Debt to Greece and Rome

EDITORS
GEORGE DEPUE HADZSITS, PH.D.

DAVID MOORE ROBINSON, PH.D., LL.D.

TURRIS
AMBULATORIA
"Walking tower"

TESTUDO
ARIETARIA
Mantlet with
ram suspended
beneath it

TESTUDO
"Tortoise"
of shields
(in center
of picture.)

ONAGER   BALLISTA
Ancient Artillery

SIEGE OPERATIONS

WARFARE
BY LAND AND SEA

BY

EUGENE S. McCARTNEY

COOPER SQUARE PUBLISHERS, INC.

NEW YORK

1963

Published 1963 by Cooper Square Publishers, Inc.
59 Fourth Avenue, New York 3, N. Y.
Library of Congress Catalog Card No. 63-10284

PRINTED IN THE UNITED STATES OF AMERICA

To

THE MEMORY OF MY PARENTS

INTRODUCTION

SOME books need no preface, and I believe this work of Mr. McCartney is one of them. However, an expression of commendation, by one whose profession is military, of a work on a military subject by a layman, may not be amiss.

The author has presented us with a book that should be appreciated by those who have neither the time nor the opportunity to delve into ancient Grecian and Roman military history at length. A book of this kind, following on the heels of the World War, in which Germany, a super-military nation, presumably so erudite in the principles of war, failed to win, may seem to be a gratuitous offering; and a reader may well ask, " What is there to this science of war anyway? " Germany's failure cannot be credited to ignorance of the science of war, but may be attributed more to her failure to apply it as an art and to her error in figuring that the principles of war could be applied to respective situations and a cer-

tain specific result obtained. No set of principles, no matter how meticulously applied, will
win a battle or a campaign, not unless " Dame
Fortune " is 100 per cent on our side, and
possibly not then. There must be something
more than a knowledge of science. There
must be the ability to apply these scientific
principles, in which we must include a proper
conception of what is known as " Command."

We are apt to refer to successful military
leaders as lucky gamblers, and many of the
best took the greatest chances. But these
chances were only taken after all the prevent-
able factors that might have contributed to
failure had been eliminated in advance.

Since science is the sum of all knowledge
on a given subject, we would not be actually
true to that definition did we not familiarize
ourselves with military history, even the most
ancient, from which these principles are de-
duced. The author has shown how similar in
the principles involved certain modern battles
are to those fought by Alexander, Hannibal,
and Julius Caesar. And one cannot but be
impressed, in reading this book, with the sin-
cerity of Napoleon when he delivered himself
of his 78th war maxim:

" Read and re-read the campaigns of Alexander, Hannibal, Caesar, Gustavus Adolphus, Turenne, Eugene, and Frederick; take them for your model; that is the only way of becoming a great captain, and of obtaining the secrets of the art of war."

But in reading and studying the campaigns of these great commanders from a military viewpoint, one must only be a historian long enough to become informed of what occurred and then be a soldier in drawing lessons and applying them to concrete cases.

In this the author has excelled, for he gives us enough of the history to localize the event and show the application of the principle, and then deduces the principle and shows its application to a modern battle.

The author brings out the importance of leadership in connection with command. In the days of small armies that operated under the eye of the commander, it was not so difficult to play up this important element " leadership," but in the modern armies that number hundreds of thousands of men and hundreds of guns, it is quite difficult for the commander, particularly of the larger units, to get into personal touch with his men to the same extent that Hannibal and Alexander did. But, nevertheless, where opportunity offers itself, and that opportunity can often be made, even the highest commanders should, and in the World War generally did, make themselves acquainted personally with the troops in the front line.

The evolution of military organization into its present form is but a development of the organizations of the ancient Grecian and Roman phalanx and legion; and it has only been in most recent times that the word " legion " has disappeared from the American organizations; while in our organizations it did not, strictly speaking, mean the same thing it did to the Roman, yet, nevertheless, we had in the Civil War such organizations as Hampton's Legion.

In taking up the principle of shock and fire, the author is but giving us a discussion of the principles of fire and movement, or the principle of movement. In ancient times, fire to cover movement in the attack, which culminated in the shock of physical contact, took the form of a standing barrage of arrows, javelins and other missiles, while the troops moved forward to get in personal contact with the enemy and to destroy him with the sword as we now do with the bayonet. This barrage now takes the form of projectiles from 75mm. and 155mm. artillery, machine guns, etc.

In Chapter VI, referring to the victory at Marathon, the writer gives us one sentence which should appeal to the armies of democracy:

"For the first time a free citizen-soldiery, inspired by lofty ideals and love of country, had turned back the lash-driven hordes of a military despotism."

In reading Chapter VI one sees illustrated by their application so many of our modern strategical, tactical formations that one must be convinced that strategy and tactics have undergone very little change, particularly the former, and the latter only in so far as to adapt itself to modern weapons. In the World War it was some time before the Allies awoke to the fact that the principle of concentrating masses against the enemy at some one point was still as good as when Theban Epaminondas applied that principle at the battle of Leuctra, 371 B.C. We soon learned to send our reinforcements in where they could get through, which was the enemy's weakest point, and not where they could not get through, which was the enemy's strongest point. The wedge at Arbela, and the overlapping and flank attacks on other occasions by Alexander read like a preliminary to campaigns of Napoleon, and I am not sure that Napoleon in forcing the crossing of the Danube near the Island of Labou had not in mind Alexander's crossing of the Hydaspes. Surely, Hooker at Chancellorsville must have heard something about that crossing of Alexander. The question of instruction and discipline, so ably handled in Chapter IX, cannot but impress the readers with the source of the strength of the Roman soldier. Our preliminary drills with the bayonet and the grenade in our various instruction camps at the beginning of the World War could not but have impressed the Roman legionaries had they been about to see these activities, and the discipline that we tried to instill into our soldiers and in which we met with considerable success was only that form of discipline which Caesar found so necessary — that subconscious obedience to the will of the commander. Military hygiene, sanitation, castrametation, and subsistence were not unknown to Caesar, as shown in Chapter IX.

Had the spade been used at Shiloh by the Federal troops as assiduously as it was used by the Romans in protecting their camps, the Federal Army would not have come so near to an overwhelming defeat.

The Germans since the days of Von Schlieffen have been most profound in their study of the principle of the Battle of Cannae, and it was no fault of the Von Schlieffen plan which he intended should be carried out on " Der Tag," that the Battle of the Marne was a Teutonic failure. The Von Schlieffen plan in spirit was not carried out by the younger Moltke, for Von Schlieffen welcomed the French offensive into Lorraine, since it would facilitate a wide turning movement by his main striking arm through the plains of Belgium and Northern France.

One might discuss the points of this book at length in the preface, but it would be to no purpose, since the reader will find copious references and the specific illustrations from which he can extend his reading as far as he may see fit.

In conclusion, I might say that while having a full appreciation of the necessity for a knowledge of military history and a familiarity with the principles of war, the reader must never forget that the great difficulty is in arriving at a decision as to what shall be done, and then the greater difficulty is to get the orders executed. Marshal Foch has stated that the great difficulty in war is in the execution.

A poor plan well executed may be better in the long run than the most brilliant conception carried out in a half-hearted manner.

COLONEL W. K. NAYLOR, U. S. A.

AUTHOR'S PREFACE

I N PICTURING the high efficiency attained by the ancients in military science, I shall call attention, not only to first instances of maneuvers and to examples of direct influence, but also to certain analogies in modern warfare which are in some cases virtually a return to ancient practice, military atavism, so to speak.

It is with some misgiving that I introduce so many quotations into the text, yet my purpose is best served by letting military critics, ancient and modern, speak *ex cathedra*. When works are quoted merely by the author's name the title will be found in the bibliography.

I have used the manual of Vegetius on Military Science more freely than does the average writer on things military. It is unfortunate that he does not indicate to whom he is indebted for the miscellaneous pieces of information which he brings together. Most of his material was taken from or based upon authors who wrote when Roman discipline was stricter, Roman training more exacting, and the military machine more efficient than in his day. More than any other writer he gives us an insight into the German-like thoroughness with which the Roman army was trained.

Those who desire a full readable account of the equipment, organization, tactics and strategy of ancient armies will be able to find it in convenient form in Dodge's *Alexander, Hannibal* and *Caesar*, the first three volumes of the *Great Captains* series.

CONTENTS

ILLUSTRATIONS

WARFARE
BY LAND AND SEA

WARFARE BY LAND
AND SEA

I. PERMANENCY OF ANCIENT
CONTRIBUTIONS

CAN any one be so indifferent or idle as not to care to know by what means, and under what kind of polity, almost the whole inhabited world was conquered and brought under the dominion of the single city of Rome, and that too within a period of not quite fifty-three years? [1]

This question is put by Polybius, a Greek, whose country at the end of those fifty-three years, 167 B.C., was part of the Roman dominion and who was himself practically a prisoner in Italy. We of the present generation marvel likewise at the achievements of Polybius's countrymen, which reached their climax in a material way in world empire under Alexander.

It is not the province of this investigation to answer in full, even from the military side, the question put by Polybius, but rather to note advances made by the Greeks and Romans in the art of war while they were acquiring this power, and to record their lasting contributions, especially in tactics and strategy. War, even as conducted today, is to be included among the many activities of modern life which owe their first scientific development in Europe to Greece and Rome.

Greeks and Romans were not, of course, the first peoples in the world to have soldiers as distinguished from warriors. In the fourteenth century before Christ, in the battle of Kadesh, fought in North Syria between the Hittites and the Egyptians under Ramses II, tactical and strategical ability of a high order was displayed, yet this is the only very early battle the maneuvers of which can be ascertained in considerable detail.[2]

Not until 546 B.C. was there fought another engagement of whose formations and maneuvers we have a detailed record. At the battle of Sardis in which Cyrus the Great vanquished Croesus, one of the great obstacles to the consolidation of the Persian Empire, we see the first skilful attempt to coördinate shock and fire tactics.

[4]

" The javelin-men," says Cyrus, " I shall range behind those armed with corselets, and behind the javelin-men the archers; for how could any one place those in front who themselves confess that they can sustain no encounter hand to hand? But when they have those armed with corselets in front of them, they will stand; and the one line hurling their javelins, and the other discharging their arrows, over the heads of those ranged before them, will do execution upon the enemy; and as far as any one does harm to the enemy, it is plain that so far he relieves his fellow combatants." These words Xenophon records for us in the *Cyropaedia*,[3] a work throughout which we find attributed to Cyrus and even to his opponents a marked appreciation of military formations and maneuvers and principles.

Greece and Rome are the only ancient European nations that had soldiers with all that such a word implies in matters of organization and coördination and discipline. The fighting men of other nations were merely warriors, men with as much strength and heroism and perhaps as much patriotism as the Greeks and Romans, yet for want of training unable to use these qualities to the greatest advantage.

Most of us have a mental picture of the ancient soldier clad in helmet, breast-plate, greaves and shield, and equipped for the offensive with javelin, spear or sword, and perhaps a dagger. We think of light-armed active men, consisting of slingers, archers or javelin-throwers, or even the cavalry as engaging in preliminary skirmishes, while behind them advance hoplites or legionaries. We see the heavy-armed men, protected by cavalry on the flanks, fighting grimly in ranks in a stand-up finish fight in which brawn and manual dexterity gain the day. Such, in its lowest terms, is a description of the equipment and method of the ancient soldier. It may pertinently be asked what contribution he could make to the science of warfare.

Tactical methods change with the change of weapons. The invention of complicated mechanisms of destruction has made modern warfare an involved operation and in general has caused ancient methods to be discarded, so that in present-day military instruction they have only an historical interest. Tactical principles, however, are not so transitory. To-day armies may fight in the open many miles apart with mountains intervening, or a few yards away in the depths of trenches, yet the salient so common in contemporary warfare is really a logical descendant of the ancient tactical formation of the *cuneus* or wedge, and conveys the same ominous threat. Another factor that makes for the modification of tactical theories is the national temperament. A Roman could hardly be expected to fight like a Greek, or an American like a German, in spite of the fact that one nation cannot disregard what another progressive one is doing. Changes will be inaugurated to allow for the evolution of the man as well as of the weapon. Still modern tactics are in many cases a development of ancient tactics, and, as far as Europe is concerned, the Greeks and Romans must be given credit for doing pioneer work.

In grand tactics, the immediate moves which bring about the clash of armies, we shall find modern analogies to ancient situations and even instances of indebtedness. In 1851 the great military critic Jomini, when asked whether recent improvements in firearms would cause any great modifications in the art of war, replied that " they would probably have an influence upon the details of tactics, but that in great strategical operations and the grand combinations of battles, victory would, now as ever, result from the application of principles which had led to the success of great generals in all ages; of Alexander and Caesar, as well as of Frederick and Napoleon." Comparisons with the strategy of Frederick have in fact been made in a special study to explain and illustrate the strategy of Pericles.[3a]

A decade before the Great War Marshal Foch quoted with approval the words of Von der Goltz to the effect that the principles of military art are everlasting, although it deals with factors that undergo a ceaseless evolution. Material and mechanical development will not nullify principles of strategy, although it will affect the application of them. It is the practice of strategy that is elastic, and in this field, each age has its own peculiar problems to face and solve.

Not even the inventions of the last two or three decades have changed the fundamental principles of strategy. With the greatest of all wars in mind, a recent authority writes: " While this war involved greater numbers of men on both sides than any previous war, weapons of greater destructive power and

[8]

more rapid and sure means of transportation
and communication, yet the general methods
followed were like those of Thutmose III,
Alexander, and the rest. We see the same
endeavor to bring destructive forces to positions of strategic importance; the same endeavor to find the weak point, to make flank
attacks, to feint at the line of communication
or attack it; to feint at the line of retreat or
attack it; the same endeavor to hold a force
of the enemy with a part of one's own force
while dealing an important blow with another
part; the same endeavor to envelop and capture the enemy." [4]

Napoleon tells us that " Gustavus Adolphus,
Turenne, and Frederick, as well as Alexander,
Hannibal, and Caesar, have all acted upon the
same principles. These have been — to keep
their forces united; to leave no weak spot un-
guarded; to seize with rapidity on important
points."

That antiquity still has military lessons to
teach is shown by other words of Napoleon
in which he urges the aspiring general to make
war after the fashion of Alexander, Hannibal,
Caesar, Gustavus Adolphus, Turenne, Prince
Eugene, and Frederick the Great; to read and

read again the history of their eighty-eight campaigns; to use them as a pattern, the sole means of becoming a great captain. Such study, he says, will be enlightening and through it one will learn to reject all maxims foreign to those of these great commanders.

In his school-days, Napoleon is said to have sacrificed many a play hour to read works of history, particularly Polybius and Plutarch. An indication of the early ripening of his judgment is seen in his preference for Arrian's history of Alexander over that of Quintus Curtius. In his camp library were included classical authors treating of things military, such as Thucydides, Polybius, Plutarch, Arrian, Livy, Tacitus.

Even though a general has come up from the ranks in time of war, his observation and experience cannot possibly be broad enough to enable him to meet every emergency. He can, however, fortify himself by reading, and to this extent is able to prepare for war in time of peace. " On the field of battle," says Napoleon, " the happiest inspiration is often only a recollection."

It will be noticed that of Napoleon's seven great captains, there are three ancients, one a

Greek, one a Roman, one neither Greek nor Roman, but a student of Greek military history and a teacher, though an unwilling one, of the Romans. In view of his relation to both great classical races, it seems imperative to include in this volume his contribution to the science of warfare.

Of the eighty-eight campaigns, from which Napoleon says a complete treatise of the art of war could be written, embracing all the principles of offensive and defensive warfare, thirty-eight were carried on by the three ancient generals, eight by Alexander, seventeen by Hannibal and thirteen by Caesar.

In Creasy's *Fifteen Decisive Battles of the World*, which ends with Waterloo, five conflicts are ancient. We may stop to mention them, although military authorities are not in entire accord with Creasy's judgment. The first one, Marathon, 490 B.C., decided not merely that the course of empire should go westward, but that the empire should be western. In 331 B.C. at the battle of Arbela, or, as Plutarch prefers to call it, Gaugamela, Alexander ended forever the Persian peril. The defeat of the Athenians before Syracuse in 413 B.C. was decisive, according to Creasy,

in removing the menace of Athens to the independent nations of the West. The disaster to
Hasdrubal at the Metaurus in 207 B.C. made
it clear that an Aryan rather than a Semitic
civilization should dominate the world. At
Teutoberg forest in 9 A.D., a terrible defeat
was administered to the Romans by the Germans under Arminius. " Had Arminius been
supine or unsuccessful," writes Creasy, " our
Germanic ancestors would have been enslaved
or exterminated in their original seats along
the Eyder and the Elbe." The island which is
now the seat of a world empire would never
have borne the name England.

In spite of the advances in methods of warfare made by other nations, the Greeks seem
to have derived and formulated their military
art almost entirely from their own experience
in battle. Though it seems safe to assume that
knowledge of machines of war was introduced
from Persia, since, among other reasons,
Cyrus the Great had used them in his campaigns, they were probably recommended to
mainland Greeks by Asiatic Greeks who had
had painful experiences with them. At all
events, the study of the evolution of modern
warfare begins with the Greeks.

If the study of strategy could be conveniently divorced from that of tactics, it would still be possible in large measure to make ancient examples of strategical principles the basis of modern instruction.

II. THE EVOLUTION OF GENERALSHIP

THE modern idea that the general is first and foremost the intellectual leader of the army is so well established that it is hard to realize that it is an evolution from an origin far different. The Greek word for general is *strategos*, 'one who leads the army;' the old Latin word is *praetor*, 'one who goes before.' From the etymologies one would suspect that the ideal general was the man qualified to set his army an example in courage and prowess. And such the history of war shows him to have been. It is not surprising that Plutarch should make the observation [5] that from the earliest times the soldiers thought that man best fitted to rule who was most valiant in feats of arms.

How strong the conception of physical leadership was will be recognized more clearly if we recall the names of a few of the many generals who were casualties on the field of battle. The Athenian Cleon was slain in retreating from the fight at Amphipolis (422 B.C.), and his victorious opponent, Brasidas, was fatally wounded; Cleombrotus was mortally wounded at Leuctra (371 B.C.); Epaminondas died shortly after the battle of Mantinea (362 B.C.) from a spear wound he received in the breast while heading the charge, pike in hand; Philip was wounded at Chaeronea (338 B.C.); Agis was slain at Megalopolis (331 B.C.); at the third Battle of Mantinea (207 B.C.), Philopoemen completed his victory by personally slaying his opponent, Machanidas. The Persian prince Cyrus was killed at the head of his combined Persian and Greek army.

In quelling a mutiny among his soldiers, Alexander boasted that he could show wound for wound with the bravest and still have some to spare. Plutarch [6] gives a long list of injuries inflicted upon Alexander by mace, scimitar, sword, arrow, dart and spear. In the attack on the city of the Malli Alexander personally led one of the storming parties. Impatient with the progress of events, he seized one of the first two scaling ladders to arrive and led the way up. When with only three companions he had reached the top of the wall, the ladders broke with the weight of the Macedonians hurrying to his assistance. Not heeding the entreaties of his men who implored him to jump down into their arms, Alexander with his companions leaped down on the inside. Fighting desperately, he had his corselet pierced by an arrow that penetrated a lung. When it seemed that nothing could save him, his men arrived and rescued him. Thanks to a good constitution and robust health, the young king recovered.

This hair-breadth escape emboldened Alexander's officers to protest against his risking his life in dare-devil feats, but it was neither his nature nor policy to direct engagements from a position in the rear. As one writer puts it: " Napoleon used his sword once as generalissimo; Alexander was first in a breach, first in a charge, wounded a dozen times, himself the leader of every desperate expedition. Half of it was mad recklessness, the other was set purpose; professional armies were new as yet, and the machine needed animating with a personal feeling, if it were to submit to the labours which Alexander designed for its endurance." [7]

The killing of Alexander at either Issus or

Arbela would have meant the destruction of the Macedonians, yet without the inspiration of his magnetic presence and prowess in the front line, it is hard to see how these battles could have been won. Armies were not yet ready for solely intellectual leadership.

If chivalry in war ever existed, it was among the Greeks, and in the days of the Trojan War, when champions fought openly and prided themselves upon taking no unfair advantage. Homeric notions about the proprieties of battle died hard. When the Spartan Archidamus saw a dart from a machine of war that had just been brought from Sicily, he exclaimed: " O Hercules, the valor of man is at an end." On the eve of the battle of Arbela, Alexander rejected the proposal to attack by night, declaring that he would not steal a victory.

The Athenians especially took pride in the display of valor. In the funeral speech of Pericles eulogizing those who had fallen in the first year of the Peloponnesian War, we find set forth with pride a policy that seems to us to be suicidal: " In the study of war also we differ from our enemies in the following respects. We throw our city open to all, and never, by the expulsion of strangers, exclude

any one from either learning or observing
things, by seeing which unconcealed any of
our enemies might gain an advantage; *for
we trust not so much to preparations and
stratagems, as to our own valor for daring
deeds.*" [8]

Not even in Hellenistic days was there general recognition regarding the commander's
proper part in a battle. In Polybius [9] we find
a significant sentence apropos of the battle of
Mantinea in 207 B.C.: "And now there occurred an undoubted instance of what some
doubt, namely, that the issues in war are for
the most part decided by the skill or want of
skill of the commanders." In making his
plans for the battle, Philopoemen had shown
wonderful foresight, and it was only his pre-
cautionary measures that enabled him to con-
vert into victory an apparently overwhelming
disaster.

Perhaps no Greek had a clearer conception
of the intellectual side of generalship than
Philopoemen. Of him Livy writes [10] that when
he came to a place that was difficult of passage,
he would, when alone, ask himself, or if accompanied, his companions, what measures should
be taken if the enemy appeared in front, on

the flank, or in the rear. These and other questions he used to ask.

Napoleon knew Livy well, and one of his maxims of war sounds strangely familiar: " A general-in-chief should ask himself frequently in the day, ' What would I do if the enemy's army appeared now in my front, or on my right, or my left? ' If he have any difficulty in answering these questions, his position is bad, and he should seek to remedy it."

The Romans, too, seem to have had a real Homeric code of fighting. With them, war was a sort of duel (*bellum* < *duellum*), a personal encounter in which the most valiant won. For the commander who stripped off the armor of the opposing commander-in-chief whom he had vanquished in single combat, there was the reward of the *spolia opima,* ' the richest spoils.' This honor was gained but three times, although champions at times represented the contesting armies, notably in the case of the Horatii and Curiatii. Titus Manlius Torquatus and Marcus Valerius Corvinus gained both fame and *cognomina* by defeating in single combat Gauls of huge stature. During the Spanish campaigns Scipio deliber-

ated whether he should accept the challenge
of a Gaul to single combat. Marcellus never
declined a challenge and always succeeded in
killing his opponents.

Among the Romans for centuries we find
the idea of personal leadership very pro-
nounced. In the Second Punic War, many
Roman consuls met a tragic end. Flaminius,
Aemilius Paulus, and Marcellus were among
those who perished. Publius Cornelius Scipio,
the father of the destined conqueror of Hannibal, was carried wounded from the battle of
the Ticinus (219 B.C.).

At one time the Romans seem to have looked
upon strategy as base deceit or treachery. In
connection with the story of the refusal of the
Roman senate to treat with victorious Pyrrhus,
we are told that the Romans placed their dependence on heroism, and not on ruses or plot-
ting. Even Caesar, when he found it necessary to abandon the investment of Pompey's
army at Dyrrachium, imperative as it was for
him to steal a march upon his foe, still made it
a point of honor (or pride?) to sound the signal for retreat by a blast of the trumpet.
There is a significant passage in Livy,[11] in
which the historian of Rome's greatness makes

it a point of national pride that the Romans did not employ the stratagems of the Carthaginians, or the wiliness of the Greeks of that period, among whom, says our author contemptuously, it was more glorious to outwit a foe than to vanquish him with main strength.

Rome's arch enemies in this war well understood the province of the general. Polybius tells us that, at the battle of the Metaurus, Hasdrubal regarded his personal safety as of the highest importance until all was lost. Then he faced his fate, and died a death worthy of the lion's brood, the sons of Barca.

Their first real insight into generalship was acquired by the Romans during the Second Punic War. When Hannibal was addressing the men who were to form an ambuscade for a flank attack upon the Romans at the Trebia (218 B.C.), he said: "You have an enemy blind to such arts of war." [12]

After their defeat in this engagement and the colossal disaster at Lake Trasimenus (217 B.C.), they began to sense the reason for continued Carthaginian success. Subsequent to the debacle at Cannae they had a wholesome respect for this new factor in warfare. Thereafter they paid it many a tacit compliment.

Though they themselves had much better fighting material than the Carthaginians, time after time they allowed Hannibal with but a fraction of their own numbers to march without a fight up and down Italy and to pass by their armies almost unmolested. The Romans saw that they *must* take lessons from Hannibal. Under his instruction the Roman generals, especially Claudius Nero and the younger Scipio, began to execute movements they would never have dreamed of otherwise.

On one occasion during the African campaign against Metellus Scipio, Caesar was marking time at Ruspina while awaiting his veterans. His opponent, becoming emboldened, "advanced with his whole army and towered elephants" right up to Caesar's ramparts. Caesar, without leaving his tent, received reports of the moves of the enemy and gave directions how to meet them. "This is the first instance in ancient military books where a commanding general is described as managing a battle just as he would today." [13]

In an emergency, even Caesar did not hesitate to snatch a shield, and to direct the battle from the first ranks by precept and example. Unlike Alexander, however, Caesar was never

a *beau sabreur;* he was the intellectual captain. In this connection one should remember
that when Caesar began his real military career
he was several years older than Alexander was
at the end of his eventful life.

In the work of Onesander, who in 49 A.D.
dedicated to a Roman consul a work on the
duty of the general, we see a full realization
of the proper functions of the commander. He
says that the science of the general avails more
than his strength, and that a general who
fights as a common soldier is like a pilot who
leaves his post to perform the duties of a
common seaman. Plutarch expressed special
admiration for Hannibal because, although he
had been in so many battles that one wearied
of counting them, he had never been wounded.

By the time of the famous siege of Jerusalem, it was generally recognized throughout
the army that a general should not endanger
his command by taking unnecessary personal
risks, for the soldiers under Titus protested
against his exposing himself. It is given as
one of the maxims of war by Vegetius that a
leader should not personally fight except in an
emergency, or as a last resort.

Tactics and strategy had become increasingly complex so that the safety of the army depended on the safety of the general. The evolution of generalship was, then, a steady, natural, and inevitable growth. The realization that it was entirely beyond the province of a general to make a practice of fighting with weapons was a contribution chiefly of the Romans.

The lesson that antiquity teaches so clearly about the proper place for the commander has not always been heeded. Steele [14] severely criticizes the Union general at the first battle of Bull Run because, instead of setting up his headquarters somewhere in the rear and directing his army as a whole, he was " at the very front, in the thick of the battle, scarcely exercising any influence on the action beyond the sound of his voice."

A lesson in sound generalship is available to all readers of Plutarch's *Life of Pelopidas:* [15] " Therefore Timotheus was right, when Chares was once showing the Athenians some wounds he had received, and his shield pierced by a spear, in saying: ' But I, how greatly ashamed I was, at the siege of Samos, because a bolt fell near me; I thought I was behaving more like an impetuous youth than like a general in command of so large a force.' "

III. THE PHALANX AND THE LEGION

BEFORE noting further contributions of the Greeks and Romans, we shall stop to call attention to their tactical units, the phalanx and legion. The phalanx consisted of rows of hoplites, heavy-armed men, equipped for the offense with spear and sword and protected by shield, helmet, corselet and greaves. The hoplite was a spearman or pikeman whose heavy equipment restricted his effectiveness to level ground. As four-fifths of Greece is mountainous, it seems paradoxical that the hoplite was the mainstay of the Greek armies. The heavy arms and armor were designed to protect the open fields and arable valley lands, since possession of them gave an enemy control of the food-supply and consequent power to dictate peace. It will be recalled that winter campaigns were very infrequent.

Power was acquired by depth of ranks as well as by heavy weapons. The average depth of the phalanx was eight men, although it occasionally reached sixteen, even before the time of the Macedonians. As early as 424 B.C. at Delium the Theban phalanx had a depth of 25, while at Leuctra in 371 B.C. Epaminondas made his left wing about 50 ranks deep.

One ancient writer,[16] who consulted several sources of information, estimates the number of men in the phalanx at 16,384. With a depth of 16 men, this would make 1,024 files. Allowing the usual space of six feet to a man, i.e., intervals of three feet, we see that the line would stretch out over half a mile in length. In close order of battle, this space might of course be reduced, as Polybius says. We hear of phalanxes of from 10,000 to 20,000 men. Naturally the phalanx was divided and sub-divided, as is the case with our own military division.

" Many considerations may easily convince us," says Polybius,[17] " that, if only the phalanx has its proper formation and strength, nothing can resist it face to face or withstand its charge."

The spear, or *sarissa,* as the Macedonians called it, might be 21 feet long, or even 24 in Hellenistic times. Five or six rows of spearpoints would project beyond the front rank making an impenetrable barrier. The spears of the rear ranks rested upon the shoulders of men in front with their points directed upward. The formation looked like a huge porcupine with the quills pointing in one direction. The Roman consul, Lucius Aemilius, a seasoned veteran, confessed to friends at Rome that he had never seen anything more terrible and alarming than the Macedonian phalanx of Perseus.

We need not, however, suppose that the phalanx of Alexander was equipped with a spear of such length. The 24-foot *sarissa* mentioned by Polybius is possibly due to lack of imagination and tactical ability on the part of the generals, with perhaps some deterioration in the quality of the troops.

The Roman legion derives its name from the *legio*, the ' gathering ' of the clans. Their fighting at first must have lacked orderly formation and intelligent direction. According to one account, the early Romans were utterly astounded when they found their opponents, the Tyrrheni (Etruscans), organizing the attack and forming compact ranks. They showed their military bent by going and doing likewise.

The legion is a descendant of the Doric phalanx, which found its way into Latium by way of Magna Graecia. The Romans adopted and adapted it, making it far more mobile and flexible. Change in the phalanx was inevitable. Without cavalry as an efficient complementary arm, the formation of the legion had to be opened so that it alone might take the initiative; otherwise the phalanx formation was doomed to stagnation, as in Hellenistic Macedon. The history of these changes is lost, but it has been suggested that innovations were made by Camillus in order to meet the initial impact of the Gauls, who used long swords, by allowing fresh troops to advance between the contestants in the front line. Mountain wars against the Samnites may have caused other changes. By the time of the wars with Pyrrhus, the manipular legion, which is built around small bodies of men, was highly developed.

Theoretically, the legion was supposed to have 6,000 men. The century, the smallest division, consisted of 100 men commanded by a centurion. Two centuries made a company or maniple. Three maniples constituted a cohort and ten cohorts a legion. Polybius tells us that the legion of his day numbered 4,200 men, in times of emergency, 5,000.

The legion had three ranks, the second of which was designed to relieve or replace those in the front rank. The *triarii*, or men in the third rank, acted as reserves to those in front of them, although they are not reserves in our sense of the word.

The legionary was armed in much the same fashion as the hoplite. He was, however, a swordsman, and not a spearman. The spear, as a weapon for close fighting, had been replaced by a short, pointed, broad sword with two edges, which he was wont to use for thrusting and not for slashing. As a rule, the spear was hurled before the lines clashed.

Through adaptation and remodelling, the Italianization of the phalanx was so complete that its foreign extraction passed unnoticed. The best type of legion never met the best type of phalanx, nor were conditions and generalship equal when phalanx and legion did meet. At Heraclea in 280 B.C., they battled for the first time. Here, after seven indecisive clashes, it was Pyrrhus's "Lucanian oxen" (elephants), aided by Thessalian horse, that beat the Romans. At Cynocephalae in 197 B.C.,

the phalanx under Philip V, after gaining an
initial success over the legion under Flaminius,
lost the day because of its inability to maneuver over broken ground.

It is really unfair to compare the best phalanx and the best legion. They were intended
for different purposes. The Romans depended
entirely upon the legionaries for victory; in
set battles, the phalanx of Philip and Alexander was expected to hold or to engage the
opposing infantry while cavalry maneuvers
were being executed. Cavalry was the striking arm. The phalanx of Alexander does not
seem to have been at the mercy of uneven
ground. It was flexible too. At Arbela it
surprised the Persians by opening up to let
the scythe-bearing chariots through.

The legion was, however, more flexible than
the phalanx. Once the spears had been put
in position, the phalanx could not be readily
divided. The legion could act as a unit or in
parts, and maniples and cohorts could be
readily detached from it, even during an
engagement.

Unlike the phalanx, the legion could defend
itself from an attack in the rear. At Cynocephalae, one wing of the phalanx carried all

before it until it was assailed from behind. Then it was easily defeated, since "the nature of the phalanx is such that the men cannot face round singly and defend themselves." [18] In the battle with the Helvetii in 58 B.C.,[19] an attack was made upon the Romans from the rear. The third line simply faced about and met the new peril.

Some flattering tributes were paid by Rome's enemies to the organization and equipment of the Roman legion. Mommsen thus sums up the changes that were visible in the phalanx of the victor of Heraclea, when he faced the Romans at Ausculum (279 B.C.): "Pyrrhus, perceiving with the sharp eye of a soldier the advantages of the Roman manipular organization, had on the wings substituted for the long front of his phalanxes an arrangement by companies with intervals between them in imitation of the cohorts." The equipment of the legion was equally good. Hannibal fitted out many of his soldiers with weapons taken from slain legionaries.

The clash of the legion aided by horse against Alexander's formation would have been a sight for Mars. With pardonable patriotism, Livy thought the Romans would have been able to defeat Alexander if he had invaded Italy. Polybius, who saw and judged with the discernment of a soldier, had no doubt of the superiority of the legion over the phalanx.[20]

The legion and, to a smaller extent, the phalanx also, with their divisions and subdivisions, capable of maneuvering in harmony or in detachments, have proved models of efficiency. Whatever the names these smaller units may take today, and whatever their numbers may be, no modern army would dare to disregard the lessons of minute organization first taught so supremely well by Greeks and Romans.

IV. ARMY ORGANIZATION: THE GROWTH OF ITS BRANCHES

THE complex organization of an army with the coördination of its many arms is the result of a long process of evolution. Because of the mountainous character of their country, the Greeks in their earliest encounters among themselves placed almost their sole dependence on the hoplite, the heavy-armed man. Even the horseman was a mounted infantryman. They had no cavalry at Marathon. They employed it at the beginning of the Peloponnesian War, but not to decide the shock of battle. Nicias anticipated for the siege of Syracuse the need of an efficient cavalry force, since he did not wish to be shut out from the interior of Sicily by the numerous Syracusan horsemen. It remained for Alexander, however, to bring out the latent power of cavalry.

At the outbreak of the Peloponnesian War, light-armed troops were held in disdain.[21] In the mountains of Aetolia, however, Athenian forces under Demosthenes were completely defeated by agile light-armed archers,[22] who refused to come to close quarters. Light-armed men from countries which had no heavy-armed men were found to be far superior to the light-armed forces of more progressive nations which emphasized the hoplite force. Before five years of this war had elapsed, it was perfectly clear that slingers, archers, and especially peltasts were a necessary complement of an efficient army.

The heavy-armed Spartans who were trapped by the Athenians on the rough island of Sphacteria (425 B.C.) managed to defend themselves from the hoplites. They succumbed only when they were assailed from a higher position in the rear by light-armed men fighting them from a distance with arrows.[23]

The first decade of the fourth century saw the equipment, training and organization of the peltasts, or light-armed men, vastly improved under the Athenian Iphicrates.[24] In 390 B.C., with peltasts supported by hoplites, he attacked without hesitation a body of 600 Spartan hoplites near Lechaeum (the port of Corinth). His men assailed the Spartans at long range with their javelins, always retiring before attacks and picking off enemies in the disorder following their futile charges. With skirmishing tactics they wearied the Spartans and would have annihilated them, had it not been for the timely arrival of their horsemen.

This engagement exercised a profound influence upon Greece, making it clear that an army needed the auxiliary branches of the service. It demonstrated that peltasts and horsemen were essential to both the efficiency and security of hoplites.

Armies were, then, becoming more complex with the advent of the fourth century. Reading aright the lessons of the Peloponnesian War, Dionysius I of Syracuse, who organized an army having eighty thousand infantry, strove for greater coöperation of the various arms. As a modern historian phrases it, he was " the first of the Greeks to combine effectively a variety of troops, as heavy-armed, light-armed, cavalry, and artillery." [25] We shall note in the next chapter his contribution to the mechanism of warfare.

Philip was the great innovator in army organization. As early as 342 B.C. we find the orator Demosthenes noting with alarm the unprecedented warlike preparations being made by Philip and calling attention to the Macedonian peril. He says in effect: " Formerly, the Lacedaemonians as well as the other Greeks did nothing more than invade each other's territory, during the four or five summer months, with their native force of citizen hoplites: in winter they stayed at home. But now we see Philip in constant action, winter as well as summer, attacking all around him, not merely with Macedonian hoplites, but with cavalry, light infantry, bowmen, foreigners of all descriptions and siege-batteries." [26]

We shall see how he developed artillery and laid the foundation for scientific siege-craft. Attention will be directed likewise to the part cavalry played in his army. In view of Philip's passion to invade Persia, it is a warranted assumption that the experiences of Xenophon's Ten Thousand in that land had something to do with the increased complexity and greater coördination of the Macedonian armies, although in Greece itself a tendency in that direction had already become manifest. Xenophon's hoplite was infinitely superior to any Persian infantryman, but he was severely dealt with by the Persian cavalry in the plains, and fared badly at times at the hands of the light-armed mountaineer. When the Greeks again entered Persian dominions, they were prepared for all kinds of warfare.

" This scientific organization of military force, on a large scale and with all the varieties of arming and equipment made to coöperate for one end, is the great fact of Macedonian history." [27] With Philip war had become the business of the specialist.

Before Philip's time no army, not even the Spartan, was kept constantly under arms. Although there had been before his day professional soldiers, i.e., mercenaries, even in the Greek armies, and though Greeks themselves had served as mercenaries, yet he was the first leader to institute a professional standing army imbued with a national spirit and instantly and permanently operative.

Philip's untimely death left unfulfilled his hope of invading Persia, but to his genius as an organizer must go much of the credit for Alexander's achievements. Alexander inherited his father's organizing ability as well as an organized army. With his improvements and additions Greek military efficiency had reached its acme.

The Romans instituted a standing army independently of Greek influence. According to Livy, the protracted siege of Veii, which lasted ten years (406–396), caused the Romans for the first time to engage in winter campaigning, and, incidentally, to inaugurate the custom of paying soldiers. Here too was a standing professional army, but it lacked the modern aspects of complex organization and intensive training which characterized Philip's. It was not until the Second Punic War that the Roman army attained a complexity and a system of coördination at all comparable with the Macedonian. To the Greeks must be given the credit of priority in this field.

V. SHOCK AND FIRE: THE DEVELOPMENT OF ARTILLERY

THE two cardinal means of bringing force to bear upon an opponent are shock and fire. Today, with the discoveries and inventions of modern science at command, fire is in the ascendant. In antiquity the reverse was the case. No body of men ever crashed through an opposing line with greater power and momentum than did the deep-ranked phalanx.

In the Great War, the Germans especially trained 'shock' troops who were used to form a 'spearhead' in assaults. This formation is virtually a return to the wedge of antiquity. One ancient writer tells us that the Thracians borrowed this formation from the Scythians. Philip of Macedon used it so effectively that its invention was attributed to him.[28] Alexander employed it with good results, notably, at Arbela. It was used by the Romans, too, who in camp slang sometimes called it the 'hog's head.'

Shock tactics were not, however, used to the exclusion of fire in antiquity. We find ancient analogues to our small arms in hand-thrown missiles, leaden bullets for the sling, the javelin and spear. The Romans were in the habit of hurling the *pila* before the shock and of resorting to their swords after the clash of the lines. The combination of spear and sword corresponds to our use of the rifle with the bayonet attached.

The Roman method of fighting reminds one of the tactical ideas of " Stonewall " Jackson, an outstanding infantry commander of the Civil War: " There ought not to be much firing at all. My idea is that the best mode of fighting is to reserve your fire till the enemy get — or you get him — to close quarters. Then deliver one deadly, deliberate fire and — charge! " [29] His tactics were Roman with the exception of the modification due to the substitution of explosives.

Among the Greeks especially we find a device that secured the same effect as the rifling of a gun. This was a detachable thong some eighteen inches long, which was wound tightly around the shaft in such a way as to leave a loop for the insertion of a finger or two. As the missile was thrown, the unwinding of the thong imparted a rotary motion to it and gave it greater steadiness, carriage, and penetrating power. The advantage of the thong has been demonstrated by experiments carried out for the Emperor Napoleon. It was found that a javelin which could be thrown only twenty meters without it could be hurled four times as far with it.[30]

Of Europeans, the Greeks and Romans first started to make war mechanical and they seem to have developed the warfare of machinery as far as was possible without the aid of explosives. The first of these machines of war was the ram, which was nothing more than a beam or trunk of a tree with one end fitted with metal, shaped at times like a prow, or even like a ram's head. The first Athenian, and presumably the first Greek, to employ this device, was Pericles, who used it in the siege of Samos (440–439).[31] He was not, however, the inventor, since it had long been in use by older civilizations.

The beam of the *aries*, or ram, which resembled the mast of a ship, was often as much as 80, 100, or even 120 feet long. It could, therefore, reach across an intervening ditch or moat, and at the same time be operated from a position of comparative security. The Jewish historian Josephus tells us that there was no tower so strong or wall so broad that it could resist more than the first assaults. Demolition was only a question of time.

At the siege of Rhodes in 305 B.C., Demetrius, who acquired from the investment the epithet Poliorcetes, ' Besieger,' had two rams 120 cubits long. They were suspended from sheds and the moving and operation of them required the services of a thousand men. With them he battered down sections of wall containing stones four feet long.[32] A ram that the Romans used against Carthage (149 B.C.) was so large that 6,000 men were needed to bring it into action.[33] These monstrous devices demolished fortifications as inevitably as a ' Big Bertha ' crushes modern defences.

For missiles, too, mechanical forces were utilized. The new power that was brought into play was the elasticity of torsion derived from immense coils of tightly twisted sinews, strands of horse-hair, or cordage. The credit of invention must go to the Sicilian Greeks. Diodorus, the Sicilian, who is doubtless proud of the achievements of his countrymen, tells us [34] that the catapult was invented in Syracuse about 400 B.C. under the patronage of Dionysius.

The catapult and ballista had three main parts: a stout standard, a track or groove for the missile, and the twisted skeins for creating motive force. The common ammunition of the catapult was arrows, of the ballista, stones. The term ballista was used only by the Romans, but the machine indicated by it is the same as the Greek ' stone-thrower.' The missile track of the ballista appears to have rested on the ground at an angle of 45°. Naturally the lighter missiles of the catapult were shot at a lower trajectory.

These machines designed to increase the range and destructiveness of missiles are worthy of our utmost respect. Vitruvius speaks of ballistae intended to throw stones weighing from 2, 4, 6, 10, and 20 lbs. up to 360 lbs.

The engine which threw missiles with the highest trajectory, the onager, ' wild ass,' did not have a groove, but hurled stones from the end of a spoon-like holder in the end of a long wooden arm. Because of its high-angle fire, this machine is the nearest approach to the modern howitzer.[35] Its range could be increased by the use of a sling attached to the end of this arm. It has been found that a modern model which will throw an 8-lb. stone from 350 to 360 yards will, when aided by a sling, cast it from 450 to 460 yards, and when the skein is twisted to its limit of tension, to nearly 500 yards.[36]

One Greek writer tells us that some engines could throw stones, the weight of which he does not specify, 700 or 800 yards. We are fortunate in having the testimony of an eye-witness of the performances of some of the Roman machines. In *The Jewish War* Josephus states [37] that at the siege of Jotapata by Vespasian the stones made a casualty of every man in their path, no matter how deep the ranks. In the same work, he says practically the same thing about their power at the siege of Jerusalem by Titus. Some stones the Romans shot weighed a talent ($57\frac{3}{4}$ lbs.) and carried 1200 feet or more. Demetrius made a protracted bombardment of Rhodes with stones weighing a talent.

So powerful were missiles from artillery that, at the siege of Massilia, Caesar's men constructed sheds or mantlets (*porticus*) with beams a foot thick.[38]

In describing a battle fought near Cremona between the armies of Vitellius and Vespasian in 69 A.D., Tacitus [39] tells us that a huge ballista of the Fifteenth Legion would have destroyed the opposing battle line, if it had not been put out of commission by two soldiers, who braved death to destroy its mechanism.

During the siege of Syracuse (214–212 B.C.), Marcellus prepared upon a raft a huge contrivance to attack the walls from the sea. The great mathematician, Archimedes, took counter-measures. While the device was still a great distance away, it was struck by stones of ten talents in weight. The third one, which fell with a terrible crash, broke the platform on which the machine stood, loosening its bolts, and tearing asunder its supports. It has been questioned whether the Attic talent is meant here, but in general the figures of the ancients about the performances of their machines are to be regarded as trustworthy.

Modern reconstructions of Greek and Roman artillery, although falling far below the perfection of the ancient devices, have made remarkable records. " Small engines, with arms about 2 ft. in length and skeins of cord about 4 in. in diameter . . . will send a stone

[4 5]

ball, 1 lb. in weight, from 300 to 500 yards."
Some of these devices can cast " arrows, or
rather feathered javelins, of from 5 to 6 lbs.
weight, to a range of from 450 to 500
yards." [40]

Strange to say, the ancients thought about
the possibility of inventing a machine-gun.
One was in fact contrived by a certain Dionysius of Alexandria. It fired a succession of
arrows supplied by a magazine or hopper.
This ancient counterpart of the mitrailleuse
was called *polybolos,* ' repeater-thrower.' [41]

Caesar interrupts his story of the siege of
Avaricum long enough to express his admiration for the bravery of the Gauls. We shall
use the passage to show that the Romans had
a quick-firing engine: "A certain Gaul, before the gate of the town, was hurling into the
fire over against a turret lumps of grease and
pitch that were handed to him. He was
pierced by a dart from a ' scorpion ' in the
right side and fell dead. One of the party
next him stepped over his prostrate body and
went on with the same work; and when this
second man had been killed in the same fashion
by a scorpion-shot, a third succeeded, and to
the third a fourth; and that spot was not left

bare of defenders until . . . a stop had been put to the fighting." [42] Like the other pieces of artillery, this 'scorpion' presumably derived its power from the recoil of tightly twisted cordage.

In lieu of the explosive power of gas, the ancients endeavored to use compressed air. Ctesibius, an Alexandrian engineer of the third century B.C., found a means of gearing to the bow-arms of the catapult pistons working in carefully wrought cylinders.[43]

Among the Greeks of the fifth century B.C. the defense in siege operations was infinitely superior to the offense. In this period successful sieges were rare, and were not conducted with a great deal of imagination or skill. The Spartan siege of Plataea early in the Peloponnesian War is remarkable for the vastness of its operations rather than for its cleverness. It was the old passive method of blockade by contravallation.

In the next century great improvements were made in siege machines by the Syracusan tyrant, Dionysius I, and by Philip of Macedon. Such a stock of engines and projectiles as they used had never before been seen. War had taken a big step toward industrialization. So

many craftsmen were summoned to Syracuse
by Dionysius that it seemed " as if the best
engineers from all over the world had been
brought together in one place." [44]   He used
engines of war in great numbers at the siege
of Motye,[45] a Carthaginian city on an island
just off the western corner of Sicily.

The new era in siege-craft is really ushered
in with Philip's investment of Perinthus and
Byzantium in 340 B.C.[46] Perinthus, a promontory terminating in abrupt cliffs toward the
Propontis, was unassailable by sea. A high
wall stretching across a neck of land seemed
to give it equal security by land. Philip did
not, in fact, manage to take it, but in the
endeavor he used devices and machines in a
way in which they had not been employed before. From towers 120 feet high, loftier than
the walls, he galled the defenders. Sappers
undermined fortifications and rams battered
down stretches of them, so that the besieged
had to build a new wall. Artillery killed many
upon the ramparts, but the defenders returned
the fire with machines borrowed from Byzantium.[47] This is among the first artillery duels,
if it is not the very first. After a siege of con-

siderable duration, Philip had to abandon the attempt.

Philip was, then, the first to organize and equip an effective siege-train. Alexander was not slow in putting this new means of warfare to good use and in elevating siege-craft to a science.

We are fortunate in having some evidence as to the part played by artillery in the defense and capture of cities. When New Carthage was taken (210 B.C.) by the Romans, there were found in it 120 large catapults and 281 small ones, and 23 large bastillae and 52 small ones.[48] At the siege of Jotapata, Vespasian had 160 pieces;[49] in the defense of Jerusalem, the Jews had 300 catapults and 40 ballistae.[50]

In 149 B.C., as part of their plan for the disarmament of Carthage, Roman consuls forced the surrender of 2,000 catapults.[51] One authority[52] gives the number as 3,000. It is very probable, however, that many of these machines were part of the reserve supplies of Carthaginian armies and that they were taken from arsenals.

When Sulla was investing the Piraeus his

siege-train was so great that the operation of
the siege-engines called for the daily employment of 10,000 pairs of mules.[53] In an expedition against the Parthians Antony had prepared siege engines enough to fill 300 wagons.[54]

The use of artillery was not, however, confined to siege operations. It is a remarkable
thing that the first extension of its use, so far
as we can tell, was to constitute a land-battery
against ships. In 397 B.C., the Carthaginian
Himilco attempted to raise the siege of Motye
off Sicily. When he was trying to force the
narrow entrance to the harbor, catapults on
shore killed many men. This innovation with
its element of surprise created great consternation in the attacking force.[55]

Artillery was put to another noteworthy use
when Rhodes was besieged by the celebrated
Demetrius Poliorcetes. During this operation
the defenders placed three machines on ships
near the entrance of the smaller harbor to
coöperate with a land battery of two pieces in
an effort to prevent disembarkation.[56]

Alexander was the first general on record to
use artillery to protect the crossing of a river.
In his youthful campaign in Illyria he was
withdrawing his men across a river when an

attack was made by the Illyrians. He ordered engineers to shoot missiles from their pieces as far as possible. With the aid of some archers, who waded to mid-stream and shot their arrows, he covered the retreat so effectively that not a man was lost.[57] The first instance on record of the employment of artillery to cover a crossing in the face of the enemy was at the Tanais River, which Alexander's men forded to do battle against the Scythians. A champion of the enemy on the other side, having no idea of the range of the machines, approached too near and was killed. His countrymen in fear retired so far that the Macedonians crossed without much trouble.[58] On another occasion Alexander used artillery to assist in repulsing sallies made by the Indians from the citadel of Aornus.[59]

Alexander had batteries sufficiently light to be transported on the backs of animals or even of men, so that they could be used in mountain warfare. At times only the more delicate mechanism would be carried with him, since the heavier parts could be quickly constructed on the spot.

By the time of the third battle of Mantinea, 207 B.C., between the Achaean League and

Sparta, the use of artillery had become customary. As the Spartan lines deployed, catapults were placed at intervals in front of the whole force with the idea of gaining an initial advantage.[60]

How well artillery had been assimilated into the Roman army and coördinated with other branches of the service in Caesar's day, is illustrated by his line of battle against the Bellovaci in 51 B.C. His line was drawn up in such fashion that his engines could be used against the wedges of the enemy.[61]

During the Civil War when Caesar was trying to hem in Pompey at Dyrrachium, his Ninth Legion seized an elevation and started to fortify and organize it. Pompey's men took a position on a neighboring hill and by means of concentrated artillery fire forced Caesar's legionaries to withdraw. This is the first known instance of the employment of field artillery to prevent the construction of field fortifications.[62] How effective these engines had come to be is shown by the fact that in subsequent operations care was taken to keep out of range.

The Romans had very serviceable gun-carriages (*carroballistae*), as we see from the sculptures on Trajan's Column. During at least part of the Empire, a legion was supposed to have fifty-five of them. They were used both in the field and in the defense of camps. In addition, each legion had ten *onagri,* 'wild asses.' [63] Gibbon observes that the use of artillery in the field became more prevalent as personal valor and military skill declined with the Roman Empire.

Artillery was developed with reference to siege operations, but it was used in the field to such an extent that the history of the evolution of artillery tactics in Europe must begin with the innovations of the Greeks and Romans. Even a casual reading of Sir Payne-Gallwey, *The Projectile-Throwing Engines of the Ancients,* will inspire great respect for their achievements. The performances of models of his own construction have been so good that they dispel all doubt as to the dependability of ancient statements about range and power.

The same authority tells us that it is certain that if this type of engine " had survived in its perfect state the introduction of cannon would have been considerably delayed, for the effects in warfare of the early cannon were for a long period decidedly inferior to those of the best projectile engines of the ancients." In form and appearance the modern gun-carriage would seem to be a fairly accurate counterpart of the ancient *carroballista,* or field-piece mounted on wheels.

VI. GREEK CONTRIBUTIONS TO TACTICS AND STRATEGY

I N EUROPEAN tactics and strategy the Greeks did pioneer work. With that directness of vision that characterizes their race, they were able, when confronted with new situations, to see the correct solution. Each advance was only a stepping-stone to further improvement.

At Marathon, the first great battle of which we read in Greek history, we see manifested a considerable degree of tactical skill. Afraid of having his position turned, Miltiades thinned his center, made his flanks many ranks deep, and rested them upon two marshes or brooks which ran down to the sea. This use of natural obstacles may well have been an innovation in Greek military tactics. In that case the mother of the invention was the necessity, on the part of the Greeks, of neutralizing their marked numerical inferiority.[64]

Grundy, however, in *The Great Persian War* (p. 189), attributes the thinning of the center to a deliberate intention to let the Persians force their way in so that the Greek wings when victorious might attack them in flank. He claims that in the enthusiasm of victory the Greek wings could not have been restrained from pursuit if their officers had not received previous instructions about the assault upon the center. If this deduction is correct, the tactics of Marathon resemble those of Cannae and Tannenberg.

Herodotus [65] tells us that the Athenians were the first Greeks to his knowledge to charge the enemy on the run. This now seems like the only possible method of attack when forces are at close quarters, yet many things that seem simple today required a military genius to inaugurate them. Even in the Peloponnesian War the Spartans were still advancing to the attack with the greatest deliberation, with measured tread keeping time to the music of many flute-players.[66]

It is of course folly to suppose that the Athenians at Marathon, clad in their heavy armor, ran the entire distance of almost a mile. As was the case with Alexander's hoplites at the battle of Issus, they may not have started to run until they were coming within range of the Persian missiles, although at Pharsalus Caesar's legionaries did so when at quite a distance from Pompey's men. They stopped, however, of their own initiative to get their breath when the Pompeians failed to imitate their maneuver as they expected. In Plutarch's *Life of Pompey* we find Caesar stating that the impetuous rush to meet the opposing forces keys up the morale more than anything else, and that with the shouting and the excitement the courage is increased.

Whatever may be the significance of Marathon in military history, it had other results far more reaching, for it broadcasted into the world ideas that were destined to gather momentum as did the on-rushing Athenians. For the first time a free citizen-soldiery, inspired by lofty ideals and love of country, had turned back the lash-driven hordes of a military despotism. It was an ominous day for autocrats, for the train of events that it set in motion has greater power today than ever before. As if to set the seal of legitimacy upon the newborn ideas, the Greeks again vanquished the Persians, mastering their fleet at Salamis in 480 B.C. and beating back their army from Plataea in 479.

[57]

From Thermopylae onward, the conflicts of Greeks and Persians showed rather high appreciation of strategical principles. The Greeks were equipped with heavy armor for close fighting; the Persians, coming from a land where stretches of open country permitted more maneuvering and the use of cavalry, wished to avoid the Greek method. The Persians were also expert archers, and, with a little drill, could have laid down a barrage. At Thermopylae a Spartan was informed that when the barbarians let fly their shafts, they obscured the light of the sun.[67] Undaunted, he replied: " We shall fight them in the shade and not in the sun."

" In every case throughout the war in which reverse or disaster fell on either party, it was due to its having been forced, either by the nature of the position or by some tactical error of its own, into adopting that method of combat for which it was least adapted." [68]

The formation of the hollow square, which has not long been discarded, has a remote pedigree. In a campaign into Illyricum in 424 B.C., Brasidas, a Spartan general, found himself deserted by his Macedonian allies. With but a handful of men against a host, he had to effect his retreat. On the march the hoplites were formed in a hollow square, with the light-armed troops and baggage in the center for protection.[69] This seems to be the first Greek use of the formation.[70] In his initial engagement with the Syracusans, Nicias, the Athenian general, drew up half of his forces as reserves in an oblong.[71]

Xenophon developed farther the tactics of the hollow square. When the Ten Thousand were making their retreat under fire, he suggested [72] that they form a square, so that they might place the baggage and camp followers on the inside and at the same time be prepared for attack from any quarter. With the help of a specially organized body of 200 slingers and a troop of fifty horse, the Greeks managed to ward off the enemy's slingers, bowmen, and horsemen.

Strange to say, less than three generations after the experience of Brasidas in Illyria, the Illyrians themselves formed in a square as a defense against Philip's cavalry.[73] This formation was used by Alexander too.

We find Jomini, in his *Art of War*, recommending squares to oppose the enemy in plains, when he has a superiority in cavalry. The same writer says that " In the Turkish wars, squares were almost exclusively used because hostilities were carried on in the vast plains of Bessarabia, Moldavia, or Wallachia, and the Turks had an immense force of cavalry." Again he writes: " The English squares at Waterloo were only in two ranks, and, notwithstanding the heroic efforts of the French cavalry, only one battalion was broken."

" At the battle of the Pyramids Napoleon advanced in échelon of five divisional squares, centre refused, the faces being six ranks deep, with the baggage in the centre of each square, and with an interval of effective cannon range between squares." [74]

The withholding of troops from battle to act as reserves is one of the most cardinal principles of contemporary warfare. The waning months of the World War saw the commanders of titanic armies juggling their forces in an effort to use up their opponent's reserves. The value of reserves, however, has not always been so obvious. It seems to have been the idea of the generals of the fifth century B.C. to get as much weight and momentum as possible into the initial impact. With that end in view, the whole available force was utilized.

At the end of the century, however, during the wearisome Peloponnesian War (431–404), special situations began to suggest to the generals the advisability of keeping some men out of the first encounter. When the Spartan Brasidas was making an enforced retreat from Illyria, he had picked men to dash out to whatever point might be assailed.[75] These men were not reserves in the true sense of the word, since they were to engage just as soon as they could. In Nicias's first engagement under the walls of Syracuse, he placed half his army near the encampment with orders to go to the aid of any part of the army that might be most distressed.[76] Nicias carried the idea much farther than did Brasidas. This is the only instance of a genuine reserve force of which Thucydides speaks.

When Xenophon was leading the Ten Thousand toward the Black Sea, he had to be on the *qui vive* constantly to guard against surprises and ambuscades, for which the broken character of the country afforded abundant opportunity. In the country of the Bithynians, there flashed upon him the brilliant idea of detaching men from the rest of the army for emergency use. He took the three rear companies of about 200 men each and made of them three separate commands.[77]

Of this innovation Dodge, in his *Alexander*, writes: " And Xenophon is, moreover, the first who established in rear of the phalanx a reserve from which he could at will feed parts of the line. This was a superb first conception. Something like reserves had been theretofore known; but nothing so nearly approaching our modern idea." The men that Nicias kept out of battle were drawn up in a hollow square or oblong so that they lacked the freedom and mobility of Xenophon's reserves.

Naturally Alexander appreciated to the full the value of reserves. In Hellenistic times, too, Greek generals withheld some soldiers from the initial clash. At the battle of Sellasia, for instance, which was fought in 222 B.C. between the Argive Antigonus and the Spartan Cleomenes, Antigonus had as many as 2,000 men in reserve.[78]

The vulnerability of the flank was early recognized in ancient warfare, but the problem of turning it was not easy of solution. The Persian method of swinging in, somewhat in the manner of a hinge, the wing of a vastly longer line of battle necessitated a great superiority of men, or a consequent weakening of the center. Croesus's dispositions at Sardis were intended to outflank Cyrus the Great on both wings. At the very beginning of the fourth century, we find Darius at the battle of Cunaxa planning to overlap the exposed wing of Cyrus the Younger.

Greek generals put their best troops on the wings with the idea, not of assailing the enemy in flank, but of attacking opposing wings and rolling up the line. Perhaps the most striking deviation from the stereotyped hoplite tactics of the Peloponnesian War is seen in the engagement near Olpae, 426 B.C., in which allied Amphilochians, Acarnanians and Athenians fought against Peloponnesians.

The Athenian Demosthenes shared the command with the allied generals. " Fearing that he would be surrounded by the Peloponnesians, who were more numerous and extended beyond his own line, he placed hoplites and light-armed troops, numbering altogether four hundred, in a deep lane overgrown with brushwood, intending them to lie in wait until the moment of conflict, when they were to rush out from the rear on the line of the enemy where it overlapped." [79] These tactics gained a signal vic-

tory. Two years later at Delium we find horsemen, instead of hoplites, employed to make an
assault upon the rear.[80]

In summarizing the strictly hoplite tactics
of the Peloponnesian War, an astute critic of
that great conflict writes: " The hoplite phalanx was regarded as peculiarly vulnerable on
either flank. The first care of a general seems
to have been to make his front at least equal
in length to that of the enemy.[81] As to the
offensive, the indisposition to risk the flank
attack may have been due to the fact that a
body of hoplite troops engaged in making such
an attack would be liable to expose its own
flanks, since it must, under such circumstances,
be detached from the rest of the line. That
was a risk which a Greek general of the fifth
century would not undertake, and one, it may
be, that his soldiers would not face." [82] The
establishment of the principle of the flank attack by maneuver, instead of by overlapping,
was to come in the next century.

Many military innovations followed in the
wake of the efforts of Cyrus the Younger to
wrest the throne from his brother, Artaxerxes.
In 401 B.C. far within the Persian empire this
young prince with a force of 100,000 barba-

rians leavened by his Greeks engaged a force of 900,000 men. The Greek mercenaries proved victorious in their sector, but found after the battle that Cyrus had been killed and that their Asiatic allies had deserted them. Leaderless, abandoned, in the heart of a hostile country, they were in a perilous plight. In this crisis they spurned the king's demand for surrender and decided to force their way back to Greece. Thus began the famous retreat of the " Ten Thousand."

The Persian king offered a truce, agreeing to furnish supplies if the Greeks would depart peaceably. The offer was accepted, but soon thereafter five Greek generals and twenty captains were lured into a parley with Tissaphernes, a Persian general, and treacherously put to death. In this emergency, an Athenian named Xenophon advised energetic action, and, along with Chirisophus, a Spartan, was put in command. Under his leadership there followed a daring running fight to the Euxine Sea, as resourceful a retreat as history records. Foiling spies, evading ambuscades, dislodging savage foemen from commanding heights, crossing rivers in the face of vigorous opposition, devising new tactical maneuvers to meet emergencies, encountering snow six feet deep, and suffering from extreme hunger and exposure, this resourceful handful of men gradually worked their perilous way northward until, catching sight of the Euxine, the 10,000 survivors gave voice to one of the thrilling cries of the ages, " The sea!   The sea! "

Of Xenophon's feat in extricating his army, Dodge, in his *Alexander*, writes:

" Nothing like this famous retreat is known in the world's history.   Xenophon is the father of the system of retreat, the originator of all that appertains to the science of rear-guard fighting.   He reduced its management to a perfect method.   More originality in tactics has come from the *Anabasis* than from any dozen other books.   Every system of war looks to this as to the fountain-head when it comes to rearward movements, as it looks to Alexander for a pattern of resistless and intelligent advance. . . . On this retreat also was first shown the necessary, if cruel, means of arresting a pursuing enemy by the systematic devastation of the country traversed and the destruction of its villages to deprive him of food and shelter."

During the march through the country of the Carduchi, the nimble light-armed mountaineers caused Xenophon's men great annoyance by their persistent skirmishing tactics. Apropos of this type of fighting, there is an interesting paragraph in a description of the siege of Louisbourg in 1758. [83]

" Wolfe had a large corps of light infantry, picked for their marksmanship from various regiments, and trained, so far as a week or two at Halifax could train them, in tactics that became familiar enough later on, but were regarded at the time as a strange innovation on the part of the vigorous and eccentric brigadier. It was merely a matter of advancing in loose formation, and using all the inequalities of the ground for protection, coupled with a light and easy costume for the men, namely, a short jacket, small round hat, and a kind of light woollen trouser, cut moderately tight. A story goes that an officer who was regarded as somewhat learned among his fellows remarked to Wolfe that his new corps reminded him of the Carduchi alluded to by Xenophon. ' That is exactly where I got the idea,' replied Wolfe; ' only these people never read anything, and consequently believe the idea to be a novel one.' "

Only a year prior to the outbreak of the

World War a French soldier, Colonel Arthur Boucher, wrote an historical and military commentary on the *Anabasis: L'Anabase de Xénophon*. He states that it is one of the best and most exact military books that the centuries have transmitted to us and that it still has lessons for military men to ponder over and apply. He regards Xenophon as a model in working up the morale of soldiers. One suspects that Marshal Foch had Xenophon in mind when he drew his distinction between active and passive obedience. Certainly no army has displayed active obedience to a higher degree than Xenophon's "Ten Thousand," and no author suggests more ways and means to obtain it than does Xenophon in his *Cyropaedia*.

Until the battle of Leuctra, 371 B.C., which was fought between the Thebans and Spartans, it had been customary for generals to draw up their lines of battle in parallel formation. In this engagement the Theban Epaminondas wrote his name indelibly upon the scroll of master tacticians. He had about six thousand dispirited men, while the Spartans numbered some eleven thousand in the best of morale. The Theban offset this immense advantage by tactical resourcefulness. He drew up his men in oblique order with perhaps eight ranks in the center and on the right. His advanced left wing he made some fifty men deep, thus forming a narrow column of attack. It is not certain that the 'refused' part of the line advanced in true échelon order, but there is no doubt that this was the first time that a battle line assaulted in oblique order with a deliberate concentration on one flank.

The new formation gained the day and it won the battle of Mantinea, too, in 362 B.C., since the allied armies opposed to the Thebans had not yet mastered the details of the order.

A generation later we find a student of Theban tactics, Alexander, employing the oblique line to good advantage, but it reached its supreme development in the hands of Frederick the Great, who at the battle of Leuthen made a perfect échelon formation, and became celebrated for his brilliant and precise execution of this order of attack.

The massing of forces by the Theban general inaugurates a new epoch in military tactics. Before the battle of Leuctra, it was the custom to put the best troops on the right. Epaminondas, however, concentrated his own strength on his left, feeling that the right was the vital point of the enemy. It will be recalled that the obtaining of a superiority in numbers at the decisive point is the key to Napoleon's strategy. "To Napoleon the offensive implied concentrated masses hurled at the right spot; and from the start he acted on the idea of concentration." [84]

In the military career of Epaminondas, there occurs, also, the first illustration of an attempt to draw an enemy from a menacing position by attacking his capital. In 362 B.C., when his opponents were at Mantinea ready to offer the Thebans battle, he slipped away by night with the intention of taking Sparta. The Spartan army had, however, learned of the movement a little too soon, and reached home just in time to prevent the city from being taken.

The great military figure of Greece and one of the outstanding military geniuses of all ages is the youthful Alexander. As a boy, he learned the Theban theory of war; his apprenticeship he served in subduing Greece and neighboring barbarian tribes; as a master soldier he led a victorious army from one end of the Persian Empire to the other.

This heroic youth did his great work in his twenties. There seemed to be no limit to his powers, either mental or physical, as there was none to his ambition. We have already noted his unparalleled bravery. As conspicuous as his bravery was his intellectual leadership. The innovations of his predecessors he improved upon, and he made new contributions through his own resourcefulness.

Though the army organization of his father Philip was superior to any that Greece had ever seen, he managed to improve it. He likewise made good use of the tactical and strategic contributions of his predecessors. In his early campaigns across the Danube he used the square in the fashion of Brasidas and Xenophon. As we have seen, the wedge was not original with him. The value of reserves he appreciated even more fully than did Xenophon. It is said that he *established* the principle of a flank attack although he was not actually the first to use it.

The tactics that were to make Macedonia supreme were tried out by Philip in a conflict with the Illyrians. Here he engaged the whole barbarian line and held it, while he had his cavalry ride around and fall upon the flanks

of the enemy.[85] This battle displayed a
proper coördination of infantry and cavalry
and was a harbinger of future victories. In
one of his youthful engagements, that against
the Triballi, Alexander employed the same
methods.[86] Philip seems to have evolved this
method of fighting independently, although at
the battle of Delium, as we have seen, the Theban Pagondas used almost the same tactics.

Of Alexander's use of the wedge Dodge, in
his *Alexander*, writes: " Macdonald's column
at Wagram was scarcely comparable to Alexander's wedge at Arbela. For this was the
first of its kind."

The oblique march is a distinctive method
of outflanking an army. Alexander employed it most successfully at Arbela. The
Macedonians demonstrated that flanking was
possible by maneuvering. This was a great
improvement upon the Persian and fifth-cen-
tury Greek methods of swinging in the overlapping portion of a line of battle.

At present when whole nations are under
arms, instead of being represented by two or
three hundred thousand champions, it is
almost impossible for large forces to get in

the rear of the enemy. Modern enveloping movements are practically a return on a grand scale to the ancient method of turning the flank by drawing in the overlapping section of a line.

That an army has a strategic flank, the turning of which will cut it off from its line of retreat, is said to be a modern discovery. Both Marlborough and Wellington have been credited with it. Colonel Dodge, however, in his *Alexander* (p. 312), assigns this innovation to the Macedonian. At the battle of Issus, 333 B.C., Darius had taken up a defensive position upon the banks of the Pinarus River. His right wing rested upon the sea and his left was somewhat ' refused,' because of a bend in the stream.

Alexander picked out the left of the center as the weakest point, and upon it he directed his first attack. Here he gained an initial success that enabled him to menace the line of retreat of the Persians. It may possibly be argued that Alexander directed the onset upon the left for the simple reason that it was the only side that gave him a chance to maneuver. We shall, however, find the same tactics ascribed to Hannibal and to the Scipio who was destined to defeat him.

We may stop long enough to give an extended illustration of Alexander's tactics and strategy. Perhaps military history affords no better example of the use of the feint to effect the passage of a river in the face of opposition. In his invasion of Persia, Alexander had not planned to go beyond the eastern limits of the kingdom of Darius, but on reaching that point he found a pretext for venturing into the unknown land of India. Taxiles, the king of the region between the Indus and the Hydaspes rivers, surrendered to Alexander on condition that the invader should help him against Porus, king of the land to the east of the Hydaspes.

On reaching this stream the Macedonian found on the other side a powerful and resolute king whose well-equipped forces numbered, according to Curtius, thirty thousand men with eighty-five elephants and three hundred chariots. According to another estimate Porus had more than fifty thousand infantry, three thousand cavalry, more than a thousand chariots and one hundred and thirty elephants.

[74]

In addition, allies were expected whom it was necessary for Alexander to anticipate.

Though four stades wide, the river was swift and deep and nowhere could fords be seen. Wherever a crossing was even remotely possible, there Porus had stationed guards. Alexander could not cross by force and so the contest resolved itself into one of wits. To create the impression that he was going to await the subsidence of the waters, swollen by the melting of the mountain snows and seasonal rains, Alexander began to ravage the neighboring country and to bring large quantities of supplies to the bank of the river. He inaugurated a deliberate policy of making feints at crossing. He sent boats, which he brought from the Indus, up and down stream to distract the enemy. He had his men stuffing animal skins with hay, as if he were going to have them float across on them, as Xenophon's men had done on their famous retreat. Bodies of infantry and horsemen were always making their appearance at different places, so that Porus was never allowed to rest from counter-measures.

At night small detachments of horse would gather at various places, raising the war-cry and making din enough for a large force, so that Porus had to lead out large contingents toward the place where the noise was greatest and keep them there in all sorts of weather. After this experience had been repeated on numberless occasions, Porus began to relax his vigilance and to remain in camp when he heard the yelling. Porus was lulled to greater security by rumors that Alexander was waiting for the waters to subside, a piece of news that Alexander had carefully allowed to leak out.

About 17 miles from the Macedonian camp, in the bend of the river, was a wooded headland and out in the stream an overgrown island, both of which would serve to shield the movements of an army. Here the invader determined to cross. Between that spot and the camp he had patrols stationed. For many nights the sentries had been calling to one another and lighting fires. Alexander was now ready. His preparation had been as much psychological as logical.

Leaving a force confronting Porus, Alexander went to the chosen place, bent upon crossing under cover of the darkness by means of stuffed skins, rafts and boats. A heavy storm came up which at first threatened to prevent the attempt, but in the end it proved advantageous in drowning the inevitable noise of the preparations. Toward dawn the tempest died down and the Macedonians managed to embark without being detected by the sentinels of Porus. Through unfamiliarity with the region, they landed on another large island instead of the opposite bank. There was no time to take the boats around. From the island the men waded to the other side in water which reached above their breasts, and of the horses only the heads protruded.

On receiving news of the crossing, Porus, thinking that the forces were those of allies, sent forward only a small detachment under his son and this was beaten. Once across, the matchless Macedonian horse and phalanx could be depended upon to complete the victory. " This was the greatest day of Alexander's life, if we take together the splendour and difficulty of the military achievement, and the generous treatment of his conquered opponent." [87]

It would almost seem that Colonel Dodge is extravagant in declaring that Alexander's strategy and maneuvers in effecting the passage of this stream have "furnished the world with a manual of all which is most valuable in the passage of rivers in the face of the enemy." Hannibal employed quite similar tactics in outwitting the Gauls on the Rhone.[88]

While I have been unable to find any definite acknowledgments of indebtedness to Alexander's tactics at the Hydaspes, there have been many crossings of the same general character although without the elaborate psychological preparation. A military man has called my attention to the fact that at the first battle of Bull Run "Beauregard's plan was exactly the same as that of Porus, with exactly the same result; the place where the river line was really crossed was undefended. Due to the fact that McDowell was not Alexander, Beauregard escaped from the defeat that he nearly met."

The boats that Alexander used on the Hydaspes had been employed in a pontoon bridge on the Indus, from which they were brought in sections.[89] In his *Deeds of Alexander the Great* Curtius informs us that they had been used previously in the passage of several rivers. Alexander seems to have made an innovation in constructing pontoons which could be taken apart, transported and reassembled. The first really great pontoon bridges known to history are of course the ones constructed over the Hellespont for the enormous army of Xerxes.[90]

In siege-craft, too, Alexander was greater than his father. Before advancing into the Persian Empire he had to reduce the sea-coast cities on the Eastern Mediterranean. The investment of Tyre is one of the most famous sieges in the annals of mankind, if indeed it is not the most famous. In the heart of Persia, and especially on the eastern confines of the kingdom, Alexander had to subdue apparently inexpugnable hill-top fortresses, so that the mere report of their capture inspired the utmost fear in the neighboring tribes. No man was ever more fertile in ruses so essential for the art of besieging.

At the time of the battle of Marathon technical tactics and strategy did not exist; at the death of Alexander a firm foundation had been laid for the formulation of their laws.

The period of the great Greek contributions to military science is delimited by the wars

with Persia, the war in which the Great King
with an enormous host was driven back from
the diminutive land of Greece, and the war
in which the Great Captain in the character
of adventurer, explorer, avenger, statesman
and civilizer led victorious armies throughout
the length and breadth of the land of the
ancient invader.

" On the one side was a race with a war
experience greater beyond comparison than
that of any other contemporary nation; on
the other, a people whose quickness of in-
tellect rendered it peculiarly capable of sup-
plying the defects of experience by appreciation of the exigencies of the situation." [91]

VII. GREEK CAVALRY

I N very early times, the Athenians used
horses as a quick means of conveying foot-
soldiers. The first horsemen were simply
mounted infantrymen. They seem to have
been the first dragoons. The idea that a man
could fight more effectively on horseback was
of slow growth. On one occasion during the
Peloponnesian War, a contingent of five hundred Boeotian horse was accompanied by an
equal number of men trained to fight on foot.[92]
In his youthful campaign in Illyria, Alexander
gave orders, in anticipation of an engagement
with a detachment of the enemy, for half of
his horse to dismount and fight on foot.[93]

It would seem that the ancient cavalryman
with his javelin or lance was almost as well
equipped as is the modern horseman. Frederick the Great forbade the use of fire-arms
since he wished his men to rely upon the
charge at full speed, sword in hand. At the
beginning of the Great War, Uhlans were

still using long lances and the Cossacks were equipped with a similar weapon.

At Marathon, the first great battle in Greek history, neither the Athenians nor their Plataean allies had cavalry. During the entire fifth century in fact the cavalry branch of the Greek armies was not highly developed. The reason is obvious. About four-fifths of the country is mountainous and ill-adapted to horse-breeding. As a result Thessalians with their broad plains were the only nation that laid great stress on cavalry. Lack of pasturage, then, caused the Greeks in general to depend at first almost solely upon infantry.

There were, however, among the Greeks men who were especially skilled in horsemanship. Xenophon tells us that the majesty of men is best disclosed in the graceful handling of animals. It is said that there is nothing so perfect in equestrianism as the riders on the frieze of the Parthenon. The Greeks themselves are the best exemplification of their mythical creations, the centaurs, in which rider and horse are one being.

The Persians developed cavalry earlier than did the Greeks. After his defeat at Salamis in 480 B.C., Xerxes withdrew from Greece leaving Mardonius in command of a large army. In the following year the Greek forces operating against the Persians in Boeotia were receiving reinforcements and provisions by way of the passes of Cithaeron that led to Plataea. One night Mardonius sent a force of horsemen to get in the rear of the Greeks and strike at their communications. They came upon a convoy of 500 beasts carrying supplies from the Peloponnesus. This they attacked and succeeded in killing or capturing the escort and the beasts.[94] "This is probably as early a record as there is of cavalry being detached in this way to operate upon the enemy's rear." [95]

The struggle with the Persians probably showed the Greeks the necessity of developing the cavalry arm. At all events, in the next great conflict, the Peloponnesian War, we find cavalry employed in lines of battle, especially to protect the flanks. It has been estimated that prior to the time of Alexander the cavalry never averaged more than a fifteenth or a twelfth of the infantry.

It was the irony of fate that the Greeks had to display their greatest efficiency in cavalry hundreds of miles from home. In

preparation for the invasion of the Persian
Empire, Alexander greatly increased the number of horsemen. Cavalry was the choice
arm of the Persians, who had vast level
stretches over which it could act. They relied
on it so much that at the battle of the Granicus
they made the fatal mistake of using it in
their effort to prevent the Macedonian crossing. At Arbela Alexander had 40,000 infantry and 7,000 horse.[96]

Alexander's dashing, impetuous temperament naturally inclined him to the cavalry
service. With it he was apt to open battles,
and with it at the catastrophe of the drama
he was wont to appear like a *deus ex machina*.
He taught his cavalry above all things to
attack, never to await attack. He inaugurated in fact the impetuous method of attack.
He is the first European to make a practice
of using the cavalry as the striking arm while
the infantry, in this case the phalanx, made
a solid rigid resisting power.[97]

Of Arbela Denison [98] writes: " There is no
battle in history in which a better appreciation
is shown of the cavalry service, nor a better
use made of it, as well in action as in the
pursuit."

[84]

" In the use of cavalry Alexander stands without a peer. No one ever hurled his cavalry upon the enemy with such precision, momentum or effect. Its charge was always well-timed; it always won. No one ever headed horse with such god-like boldness, or fought it to the bottom as he did. Had Alexander not been one of the world's great captains, he would have been the typical *beau sabreur* of the world's history." [99]

The use of cavalry by Philip for a vigorous pursuit after the battle of Chaeronea marked a new departure in Greek warfare. One of Napoleon's maxims was as follows: " It is the business of cavalry to follow up the victory, and to prevent the beaten enemy from rallying."

We may note in general " that in the wars of Alexander, as well as long previously, light cavalry were used for outpost duties, that scouts were used for reconnoitering, and patrols and sentries and videttes seem to have been employed very much upon the same general principles as are in use at the present day." [100]

The greatest modern advocate of the cavalry arm was Frederick the Great. He is said to have found in the celerity and *élan* of the Macedonian attack a model for his own horsemen. He too taught that the offensive was the only proper sphere of action for cavalry. Like Alexander, he made the cavalry a striking arm. It is estimated that of the twenty-two great battles that he fought, his cavalry won at least fifteen.[101]

VIII. THE MARTIAL SPIRIT
OF ROME

THE Romans had their own explanation of the way in which their genius was directed into military channels. One day when Romulus was holding a review of the army, a great storm arose accompanied by loud crashing of thunder. The king was veiled in a dense cloud and snatched from the gaze of the assembled people. During the mourning of the people, who now looked upon him as a god, king and father, rumors began to spread that his body had been torn apart by the city fathers. At this juncture an influential Roman stepped forward and thus addressed the people: "Romulus, my fellow citizens, the father of this city, at dawn today suddenly descended from heaven and revealed himself to me. When filled with awe I stood in reverent attitude, invoking heaven's consent to look upon him face to face, he exclaimed, 'Go, tell the

Romans that it is the will of the gods that my Rome shall be the capital of the world; therefore let them cultivate the art of war and realize and tell posterity that no human power can resist the Romans by arms.' With these words he departed on high." [102]

Roman citizens were called Quirites. One of the suggestions for its etymology is that it means " spearmen." The legionaries of Caesar's day were swordsmen, but their ancestors were spearmen. The Quirites of early Rome were spearmen in fact, if not by etymology. In the old litanies it was upon the *pilumnus poplus* (=*populus*), " spear-armed body of warriors," that the blessing of Mars was invoked.[103]

A clear etymological indication of the martial proclivities of the Romans is seen in the word *virtus,* ' manhood.' The most obvious way to show one's manhood was by courage in battle and hence the word came to mean bravery, ' spunk,' ' grit.' Roman writers and speakers never tired of extolling heroism and heroic ancestors.

How dominant the martial spirit was in the Romans is well shown by an incident in Caesar's campaigns in Gaul. At Vesontio,

PLATE II

Roman Legionaries on the March

From Cichorius, *Die Reliefs der Traianssäule*

when he was endeavoring to allay fear of the Germans under Ariovistus, he practically asserted that the terms ' Romans ' and ' soldiers ' were synonymous. " Whenever," said he, " any one declares that it is not incumbent upon us to war, he might as well state that it is not necessary for us to amass wealth, or to rule others, or to be freemen, or to be Romans." [104] Cicero [105] practically says that the Roman soldier looked upon his shield, sword, and helmet, as being just as much parts of his body as were his shoulders, his limbs, or his hands. Josephus [106] tells us that weapons were, so to speak, a part of the physical constitution of the Roman soldiers and hence they never had any respite from martial exercises.

We learn from Livy that at the battle of Lake Trasimenus the Romans fought with such spirit that they failed to notice an earthquake as severe as those which waste great sections of Italian cities, or divert rushing streams from their courses, or dash the sea up into the rivers, or crumble mighty mountains. This is the incident referred to by Byron:

" And such the shock of battle on this day
And such the frenzy, whose convulsion blinds
To all save carnage, that, beneath the fray,
An earthquake rolled unheedingly away."

The very language of the Romans reflects their martial character. Quintilian [107] harps upon the fact that Caesar spoke in the same manner that he fought. His diction was that of a military man.[108] The organization of an involved Latin sentence, with its respect for rank and superiority, is military in character. An " unmistakable note of discipline and subordination manifests itself in the orderly way in which the Romans carry out the sequence of their tenses, all dependent tenses being subordinated to the main clause; and it again comes out in the preference shown by Latin for dependent speech, in which sentence after sentence, and clause after clause, are set under the strict *régime* of a single governing verb, as soldiers under that of a general. . . . Just as soldiers in a regiment keep their eyes fixed on their commander, all the pronouns in *oratio obliqua* (' indirect discourse ') which have reference to the speaker, look back to him." [109]

The Latin marshals its sentences like soldiers and " periods succeed each other with dignity and in well-marked cadence — spirited and irresistible like the Roman legionary. Their entire colouring recalls to us the picture of his weather-beaten face, and their stately march reminds us of his proud and masterful bearing. In fact, this well-matched pair, warrior and language, have stepped forth from their home in full consciousness of victory, and have overcome the world between them." [110]

But seldom among the Romans did " grim-visaged war smooth his wrinkled brow." The temple of Janus, whose open gates indicated symbolically that the god had taken the field with the armies, was closed but three times. Livy [111] well sums up the military character of the Romans: *Ea est Romana gens, quae victa quiescere nesciat,* " Such is the temper of the Roman nation that it knows not how to remain at peace, vanquished though it be." It was a boast of the Romans that, though defeated in many a battle, they never lost a war. [112] For them, *Vivere est militare,* " Life is a battle," was true literally as well as figuratively.

It is not strange, therefore, that among the most famous lines in Latin literature, is the passage in the *Aeneid* glorifying the martial spirit:

" Let *others melt and mould the breathing bronze*
  To *forms more fair, — aye! out of marble bring*
  Features *that live; let them plead causes well;*
  Or *trace with pointed wand the cycled heaven,*
  And *hail the constellations as they rise;*
  But *thou, O Roman, learn with sovereign sway*
  To *rule the nations. Thy great art shall be*
  To *keep the world in lasting peace, to spare*
  The *humbled foe, and crush to earth the
      proud."* [113]

IX. ROMAN DRILL AND
DISCIPLINE

THAT the Romans clearly understood the source of their strength is readily understood from one of the introductory sentences in Vegetius: [114] " We see that the Roman people have conquered the world by nothing other than drill in arms, camp discipline, and experience in campaigning." The Gauls surpassed them in numbers, the Germans in height, the Spaniards in strength, the Carthaginians in craftiness and resources, the Greeks in the sharpness of their wits, yet the Romans were able to beat them all because of the thorough and rigorous training they gave their recruits, their meticulous attention to the smallest details, and the business-like manner in which they provided materials of war. Results that the Greeks achieved by inspiration, the Romans gained by labored effort. They made war as much a business as an art.

The Romans were very modern in leaving

to chance nothing that could be anticipated. Vegetius has left us a fairly comprehensive account of the training of a Roman army. Great care was taken in the selection of material for soldiers. Enlistment officers were to see to it that recruits had alert eyes, a head carried erect, a well-developed breast, a moderate girth, muscular shoulders, strong arms, rather long fingers and sinewy legs. When these requirements were complied with, no emphasis was laid on height, since it was regarded as important for the soldier to be strongly built rather than tall. Tall men were in demand, however, for the front cohorts of the legion or for cavalry detachments upon the wings.[115] Men who had led an active life were preferred. While nothing so formal as an intelligence test was given, an effort was made to get recruits who were mentally alert as well as physically sound.[116]

One might suppose that the specialized bayonet drill of the last war has no counterpart in antiquity, but one is surprised at the thorough training given the ancient soldier in the use of the sword, which is after all much like our bayonet in that it was short and was regularly employed for thrusting and not for slashing. The 'rookie' (*tiro*) was given a wicker shield and a wooden foil, both of them twice as heavy as those used in battle. A wooden stake, projecting six feet from the ground and set so firmly in it that it would not yield, was his imaginary enemy. This he vigorously attacked, aiming at the head, as it were, or ribs, or legs, or hough, yielding ground and leaping forward as against a real opponent, and assailing it with every manner of attack. Special stress was laid on teaching the rookie to attack in such a way as not to expose himself to a counter-thrust. To this drill he was subjected both morning and afternoon.[117] Gladiators too were taught in this fashion and Vegetius knew of no champion swordsman who had not been so trained.

Since a slashing blow was often parried or stopped by bones without resulting in death, thrusting was taught as being more deadly. In addition, the thrust is more insidious and does not expose the right arm and side as does the sweeping blow. The wooden weapons were made extra heavy so that when the tiro got real weapons he would leap to the attack with greater alacrity, feeling that he had been freed from a heavy burden.[118] From this

[95]

brief description it can be seen that the Roman omitted nothing that would tend to make a more efficient swordsman.

The recruit was taught marksmanship by throwing missiles at a stake.[119] Bowmen and slingers used to set as a target bunches of twigs or straw at a distance of 600 feet. Slingers were drilled to whirl the sling around the head only once before throwing the missile. Perhaps this was intended not merely to secure greater rapidity of fire, but also to reduce casualties.[120] During the American Civil War many soldiers were wounded while they had their arms raised in using the ramrod. In anticipation of emergencies, the ancient soldier was taught to throw with the hand alone stones weighing a pound.[121] This would seem to be an ancient prototype for the grenade.

The legionary was drilled in cutting down trees, carrying burdens, leaping over trenches, swimming in the sea or in streams, walking at double pace or running under arms and encumbered with baggage, so that daily practice in times of peace might anticipate the needs of war. Training was maintained in stormy weather even if a shelter had to be improvised with a roof of reeds or sedge-grass. On days when snow and rain ceased, drill was held in the open. Even veterans had to take some drill daily for a veteran out of condition was looked upon as a recruit. An effort was made to inspire confidence in the soldier by thoroughly familiarizing him with all the conditions of battle that could be anticipated. In a battle, knowledge and experience avail more than strength, says Vegetius, and a soldier without training in arms is not different from a barbarian.[122]

Marches were taken over every kind of country and every effort was made to harden the soldier's muscles and constitution. In order to give the recruit a thorough training, sham battles were fought on the Campus Martius, and no pains were spared in reproducing the conditions of actual warfare. As Josephus admirably puts it, their drills were bloodless battles and their battles bloody drills.[123]

The Romans were keenly alive to the necessity of guarding the health of the soldiers. It is only increased scientific knowledge that makes modern armies more careful. Vegetius [124] tells us that the health of the army should be maintained by all possible precautions, that is by careful selection of camping sites, attention to the water, to the seasons, by medical care and by exercise. The soldiers should not be compelled to stay in pestilential places near disease-breeding swamps, nor in arid regions without shade-trees, fields, and hills, nor should they be without tents in summer; they should not set out on the march so late in the day as to become ill from the heat of the sun and the fatigue of the route, but rather they should start the march before daybreak and stop in the heat of the day; nor should they in a severe winter march in snows or frosts by night; they should not have to suffer from lack of fuel or clothing; for a soldier who has to shiver is hard to treat and is not in condition to make a campaign. The army should not use contaminated water nor swamp water; for impure water, just like poison, causes diseases among the drinkers. Military men have concluded that the daily exercise in arms does more to maintain the health of the army than do the doctors. For this reason they wanted the soldiers to drill under shelter on inclement days, outside on clear days. In like manner they ordered the horsemen to train both themselves and their horses diligently not only on level ground but also on steep places, amid trenches and very difficult paths, so that they might not encounter any unfamiliar problem in actual battle. From this one can see how the army must ever be getting more instruction in the use of arms, since inuring them to exertion can bring both health in camp and victory in battle. If in the summer or fall the army has to stay rather long in the same place, very dangerous diseases may arise from contaminated water and from the tainted atmosphere. This can be prevented only by a frequent change of camping grounds.

The little manual of Vegetius is extremely interesting in showing the German type of thoroughness and attention to detail that existed in the Roman army.

The veteran soldier of Caesar's day had become such an automaton of efficiency that he could in an emergency comport himself as well as if he were officered by others. On one occasion in particular the ability of Roman soldiers to act for themselves was of great value to them since it offset the advantage the Belgae derived from a surprise attack.[125] As

Vegetius says, soldiers do without alarm in battle that which they have been in the habit of doing in sham-battles on the drill-ground.

As the battle of Pharsalia was about to start, Pompey ordered his men to remain still in order to allow Caesar's legions to exhaust themselves by running twice as far as they had expected, yet when the seasoned veterans of Caesar saw this move, of their own accord they stopped midway to regain their breath.[126]

At the present time in America we are indiscriminately calling every soldier who was enlisted in the World War a veteran. In antiquity it was not so easy to get such a distinction. In Hirtius's postscript to the Gallic War [127] we find this significant sentence: " Three veteran legions conspicuous for valor, the 7th, 8th and 9th, he had with him; the 11th, composed of picked young men of the greatest promise, which, though in its eighth campaign, had not acquired the same reputation for experience and bravery." Eight years of fighting, twice the duration of the World War, and still suffering by comparison!

The martial strain, then, was dominant in Roman character and the great lesson that the Roman had to learn (*discere*) was discipline (*disciplina*). The Romans accomplished much by bravery, but even more by discipline. The earliest fighters of Rome were warriors; by the time of the Punic Wars they were well-drilled soldiers. The first fighting force was a *legio*, a gathering of the clans; the last was an *exercitus*, a body of men who had been trained. The great contributions of Rome to military science were organization, discipline, attention to details, far-sighted preparation, the realization that battles could be won before they were fought.

X. THE SPADE IN THE ROMAN ARMY

IN view of the developments of the World War, it is a very remarkable thing that the use of the spade was so fundamental in Roman warfare. High-angle fire and powerful explosives have put the modern soldier in the trench, whereas for ancient conditions of warfare, with the comparatively low trajectory of missiles, the embankment or rampart made of material excavated from the trenches afforded sufficient protection. 'Digging in' was a regular part of the day's task for the legionary. A Roman army on the march entrenched every night.

Under some conditions Napoleon recommended similar action, as we learn from one of his maxims: "In a war of march and maneuver, if you would avoid a battle with a superior army, it is necessary to entrench every night, and occupy a good position. Those natural positions which are ordinarily met with are not sufficient to protect an army

PLATE III

Roman Legionaries "Digging in" and Fortifying

From Cichorius, *Die Reliefs der Traianssäule*

against superior numbers without recourse to art."

Napoleon's conqueror, as well as Napoleon himself, gleaned lessons of military value from Caesar. In *Reminiscences and Table Talk of Samuel Rogers* [128] there is preserved for us an acknowledgment of indebtedness by the Duke of Wellington: "Had Caesar's *Commentaries* with me in India, and learnt much from them, fortifying my camp every night as he did."

According to one ancient authority, [129] the trench of an ordinary encampment should be 9 feet wide and 7 deep if there seemed to be no immediate danger. When there was a menace from the enemy, the width should be increased to 12 feet and the depth to 9. The excavated material thrown out at the side increased the total depth several feet. Caesar [130] mentions a trench 15 feet wide from which was made a rampart 10 feet high and 10 feet wide. For a permanent camp, the width of the trench should be 9, 11, or 13 feet, and, in case a large force of the enemy was near, 17 feet. [131]

Even these measurements were exceeded. Colonel Stoffel, who has done so much for our knowledge of Caesar's campaigns in Gaul, speaks of finding in the trenches around the site of ancient Gergovia coins and other remains of Roman occupation as far down as 15 feet.[132] At Alesia there was a trench or moat 20 feet wide. Trenches were used, then, not only to protect camps, but to besiege cities, so that Varro could rightly say that the Roman conquered by sitting still.

The largest trench of antiquity was, perhaps, the one constructed by Crassus during the servile uprising to shut up Spartacus and his followers within the peninsula forming the toe of Italy. From sea to sea across the neck of land over 34 (English) miles broad he ran an entrenchment fifteen feet deep and fifteen feet in breadth.[133]

It is worth while to stop to note the methods employed by the French officer in locating Caesar's entrenchments. Wherever from literary evidence and on *a priori* reasons he suspected Caesar's lines might have run, he dug trial transverse trenches, so that they would cut across any old trenches. The intersections of trenches were readily recognized by the clear V-shaped profiles made by the lines of contact between the undisturbed and the made earth.

In the use of the spade and the creation of obstacles, the siege of Alesia by Caesar [134] is the most memorable in antiquity. This great natural stronghold of the Gauls was situated on the summit of a hill so high that it was inexpugnable except by siege. At its foot on the northern and southern sides ran two streams. As the space between the brooks on the west gave the inhabitants the best opportunity to attack, Caesar built across it an immense trench twenty feet wide with vertical sides instead of the more usual tapering ones.

Farther back from the town were two other trenches fifteen feet wide and fifteen feet deep, one of which continued its course around the town as part of a line of contravallation eleven miles in extent. Outside of this was constructed a rampart surmounted by a palisade, the total height of which was twelve feet. From the rampart projected breastworks consisting of a tangle of stout branches. At frequent intervals wooden towers were erected.

To guard against sallies from the besieged

he built in front of the town a series of trenches five feet deep. According to the interpretation of our best authority on Caesar, " five rows of strong boughs were fixed in each, with one end protruding above ground, sharpened and with the branches projecting so as to form a kind of abatis." These branches were dubbed in camp slang *cippi*, ' boundary posts,' from their resemblance to surveyors' markers.[135]

In front of all these defenses there were arranged in checkerboard fashion cone-like holes into which were set sharp stakes projecting not more than four finger-breadths. The holes were concealed with brush. There were eight rows of these pits, which the soldiers dubbed *lilia*, ' lilies,' because of the way they spread out from a point. Almost identical with them are the wolf-holes constructed before Ypres by the Germans in 1914. The system of fortification ended with barbed pieces of iron, called *stimuli*, ' goads,' in soldier argot, which were set in pieces of wood implanted in the earth.

In anticipation of an attempt by the countrymen of Vercingetorix to raise the siege, Caesar constructed a circumvallation with the same defenses, but in reverse order. This was fourteen miles long.

At Dyrrachium in the Civil War, Caesar used earthworks to enclose Pompey's men and the Pompeians constructed defensive works against them. Both sides exerted their ingenuity to the utmost. Caesar tells us [136] that this was a new and untried method of warfare and comments especially on the number of redoubts and the extent of the fortifications. Dodge [137] pays his respects to these operations: "It was on the terrain thus enclosed that there were constructed the most remarkable fortifications in antiquity."

In giving a summary of the development of the art of fortification, a pamphlet prepared since the close of the Great War under the direction of a major general of the United States Army says: "From the description Caesar gives of the defenses he erected (e.g., at Alesia and Dyrrachium), it is evident that he was thoroughly familiar with all the essential principles of fortification, and with the function and use of obstacles we now know, except the wire entanglement." [138]

The maze of barbed-wire of the recent war is but an improvement upon the palisades and brushwood entanglements of the Romans. Stakes and branches were at times so closely interlaced and so firmly secured that it was impossible to insert the hand and pull them away. The Greek Polybius,[139] struck by the great contrast between the efficiency of the Roman devices and those of his own country-men, concludes that of all the military arts of the Romans their method of palisading and interwining branches is the one most worthy of admiration and imitation.

Spade work, especially when assisted by stakes and branches, was, therefore, just as effective in antiquity as it is today. Even Hannibal had to desist from the attempt to break through the defenses made by Mar-cellus before Capua. He had as much respect for fortified positions as had the British regulars, later on, after they had charged against the hastily constructed Colonial earth-works and entrenchments at Bunker Hill. In the civil wars, Roman generals regarded forti-fied positions as all but unassailable. Cae-sar refrained from attacking the camp of Scipio in the African campaign.

Sapping and mining are other ancient forms of warfare to which modern armies have resorted. In antiquity they were restricted to siege operations. Alexander had with him on his Persian expedition men who were especially skilled in these arts.

If we may believe Roman tradition, the city of Veii was taken after a ten-year siege by a tunnel which admitted the Romans to the heart of the citadel. Undermining walls beneath the protection of mantlets or moving towers was a regular part of siege operations. Counter-mining too was practised.

The best illustration, perhaps, of these tactics is seen in the siege of the Greek city of Massilia by Caesar's forces under Trebonius in the Civil War. When some thirty mines were being driven forward toward the walls, " the people of Marseilles, distrusting the entire moat in front of their wall, lowered it by digging it deeper. Thus all the mines found their outlet in the moat. In places where the moat could not be dug, they constructed, within the walls, a basin of enormous length and breadth, like a fish pond, in front of the place where the mines were being pushed, and filled it from wells and from the port. And so, when the passages of the mine were suddenly opened, the immense mass of water let in undermined the supports, and all who were within were overpowered by the mass of water and the caving in of the mine." [140]

From the illustrations already given, it is clear that the Roman used the spade to good advantage. Behind his trench and other obstacles, the Roman legionary felt even more secure than did the modern soldier in the Great War. Even hastily constructed entrenchments were looked upon with wholesome respect by attacking generals.

XI. ROMAN CONTRIBUTIONS TO TACTICS AND STRATEGY

THE Latins who settled on the hills of Rome seem to have differed from the neighboring tribes of central Italy chiefly in their capacity to assimilate. Their army was at first merely a *legio*, a gathering of the clans, and their first warlike activities were simply forays. In spite of the far-reaching reorganization of the Roman military system said to have been instituted by Servius Tullius, the sixth king of Rome, raids seem to have characterized their warfare from the time of Romulus to the siege of Veii.

In Livy's description of the battle with the Gauls at the Allia in 390 B.C., the Romans are represented as being familiar with tactics infinitely superior to any they used until the middle of the Second Punic War. He says that the Romans stationed reserves on a piece of rising ground, and that Brennus feared it was the Roman purpose to use these after 'the lines had clashed to make an attack upon the

flank and rear.[141]   If the Romans at that time
knew as much as this, then Roman generalship soon went into a Rip Van Winkle dor-
mancy from which it did not awake for over
175 years.

An incident in Roman legendary history
provided a German, at a time in the Great
War when Germany had only three big
avowed enemies, with an illustration that enabled him to drive home a point in strategy.
" Germany ought," thought Helfferich, " to dis-
pose of her enemies, like the last of the three
Horatii, who in the story defeated the three
Curiatii who were attacking him, separating
them by a clever retreat." [142]

Perhaps the only striking tactical maneuver
made by a Roman general during the First
Punic War was executed just outside of the
walls of Panormus (Palermo) in 251 B.C.[143]
The consul Caecilius lured the Carthaginians
up to the very walls by means of skirmishers.
At a propitious time he led his maniples from
the gate opposite the enemy's left and charged
them diagonally on the flank.   This move reminds one of Alexander's oblique march upon
the Persian flank at Arbela.   One suspects,
however, that this alignment was forced upon

Caecilius by the character of the terrain rather than evolved by any superior tactical skill.

The outstanding military achievement of the Romans prior to the Second Punic War was the organization of their " division," so to speak, the legion. The Roman legionary was then the best fighting material in the world and he had the best equipment. Generalship had not, however, kept pace with him, thanks to lack of imagination and the belief that main strength and discipline were the only deciding factors in battles. We have already noted Hannibal's contempt of Roman generalship just prior to the battle of the Trebia.

In discussing Roman tactics and strategy, it would be not only unfair, but impossible to disregard Hannibal, the Carthaginian patriot, whom Livy excoriates, but for whom he cannot entirely conceal his admiration. We have already had occasion to note that it was Hannibal who opened the eyes of the Romans to the real meaning of generalship. In conformity with their policy of adopting whatever superior equipment they found in the hands of foreigners, the Romans after Cannae

[113]

assimilated what they could of Hannibal's tactics.

It would seem that until the Second Punic War (218–201 B.C.) the Carthaginians knew even less of tactics and strategy than did the Romans. In 255 B.C. a Roman army of occupation had utterly defeated and cowed the Carthaginians. So sure was Regulus of his ability to capture Carthage that he undertook to dictate a ruthless peace. In sheer despair the Carthaginians refused. At this juncture, there was brought to Carthage a soldier of fortune, Xanthippus, a Spartan. He showed the Carthaginians that their defeat was due to blundering generalship. With more skilful tactical dispositions under his leadership, the Carthaginians inflicted a crushing defeat upon the Romans.

Yet only forty years after their wretched exhibition of generalship, a commander of Carthaginian extraction was roaming at large in Italy, unable to find a Roman army that would meet him in the open field. There is every reason to believe that he too profited by Greek lessons.

When Hannibal was making his final preparations to march against Italy, he took measures to protect Africa from an attack by way of Sicily, and to ensure the loyalty of Spain. Accordingly he sent Spaniards to guard Africa and Africans to garrison Spain, so that there would not be too much coöperation between garrison and people. In the same way during the period of the greatest expansion of the Roman Empire, recruits from one part of the Empire would be stationed in another in order to prevent undue sympathy between garrisons and inhabitants. One is reminded of the case of Switzerland in the Great War. It is said that she sent French-speaking soldiers to guard the German frontier and German-speaking troops to protect the Italian border.

At the Rhone in 219 B.C., Hannibal found his passage blocked by the Gauls on the farther bank. He sent a detachment a day's journey up stream with instructions to cross by night and to attack the Gauls from the rear while he himself essayed a crossing in front.[144] This method is suggestive of Alexander's tactics at the Hydaspes, though it may be only a coincidence.

Hannibal understood as clearly as did Alexander the necessity of securing his communications. This was no easy thing to do in Gaul, on account of the numbers and fickleness of the inhabitants, yet Livy [145] says that he left no unconquered tribes behind him.

In the fall of 219, after an unprecedented conquest of the snowy barriers of the Alps, Hannibal took up such a position near Placentia, to which the consul Scipio had retired, that he severed Scipio's communications with Tiberius Sempronius, the other consul, who was hurrying up with assistance. It has been denied by a French military critic that Hannibal intended to separate the armies of the Romans and then beat them one at a time. If such was his purpose, to effect strategical penetration, clearly Polybius, an extremely astute military writer, did not understand the significance of the move.

Napoleon, however, seems to have had no doubt of the meaning of the Carthaginian maneuver. Of his strategy in 1796 in taking up a central position between his opponents in Northern Italy, he says: "I was in a position more favorable than Hannibal's. The two consuls had a common interest, to cover Rome; the two generals that I was attacking had each a particular interest that dominated them: Beaulieu that of covering Milan; Colli that of covering Piedmont." Dodge [146] characterizes Hannibal's move as "crisp and masterly," and sees in Napoleon's words an acknowledgment of the source of inspiration for this stroke.

At the battle of the Trebia (218 B.C.), Hannibal engaged the Romans with a frontal attack. After the engagement had started, he set upon the Romans with a cavalry force that had been lying in ambuscade upon their right. Of this method of attack Gilbert [147] says with all the emphasis of italics: "*It remained for Hannibal to establish the true principle of a flank attack combined with a frontal attack.*" He points out that Alexander's flank attack by an oblique march is not free from certain inherent tactical defects and regards Hannibal's flank maneuvers as a marked advance.

When Hannibal was making his way south from northern Italy in 217 B.C., he learned that his way was blocked at Arretium by the consul Flaminius. Instead of coming to battle, he made a precarious passage across the marshes of the Arno, went around the left flank of the Roman, and cut him off from his communications with Rome. Here again, Dodge [148] informs us, is a clear conception of the enemy's strategic flank.

One of the world's masterpieces of battle tactics is Cannae, which was fought on the Aufidus in Southern Italy in 216 B.C.[149] Hannibal drew up his forces in the shape of a crescent, as Polybius tells us. His center was rather thin and gave way gradually before the fierce onset of the Roman legionaries. Gradually the line straightened, but not even then did the center stop. It continued to yield and the enthusiastic legionaries followed into the hollow of the sagging line. Hereupon Hannibal's wings closed in and the Romans were trapped. The disaster was completed by the return of the cavalry which, after putting to flight the Roman horse upon the flanks, assailed the Romans from the rear. Such, in brief, were Hannibal's tactics at Cannae. "No battle in history is a finer example of tactics than Cannae." [150]

This conflict has been the subject of the most intense study by the German military staff. By them it is considered a model battle. Among the most important books of General Count von Schlieffen, whom Ludendorff calls

" one of the greatest soldiers who ever lived,"
is one called *Cannae*. Upon the basis of this
ancient battle he worked out his own theories.
" Schlieffen believed in retaining the enemy's
centre, or even yielding to him a little there,
while outflanking and enclosing him on both
wings. A victory of the Cannae type, he held,
was the only sort which would ensure the
annihilation of an opponent." [151]

By him was conceived a German plan of
campaign to be put in operation on the West
Front in case of a war with France and Russia.
With his elaborate enveloping movement
through Belgium in mind,[152] Admiral von
Tirpitz, in his *My Memoirs,* says of the Great
War prior to the battle of the Marne: " Until
then the army had been animated by one idea:
Cannae." The best exemplification of Cannae
is the battle of Tannenberg, which was fought
in August 1914 by Hindenburg, one of Count
von Schlieffen's pupils.[153]

He engaged the invading Russians with
retiring bodies of troops to delude them into
the belief that they were pushing through
weak opposition. " Suddenly (August 26) the
Russians, advancing on a wide front, en-
countered serious resistance. They had come

to the prepared trap of Hindenburg. At first the center seemed to yield, and the Russian general pushed forward. Then there was pressure from the south on his left. Sending troops to overcome this, Samsonoff was surprised by a wide sweep of strong German forces on his right flank.[154] For two days the Russians fought desperately against systematic attacks that closed in around their doomed army. On the third day Samsonoff was practically surrounded, his troops in a bewildering tangle of undergrowth, and his army a demoralized mass struggling in confusion. The fighting was protracted, but only the débris of an army escaped from the deadly circle. It was one of the few cases in history of the complete destruction of an army in battle." [155]

The double turning movement, the object of which was the envelopment of the Russians, had achieved for the Germans the same results that Hannibal gained at Cannae. Tannenberg is already considered a classic by military students. It is a striking fact that the only victory of the World War which resulted in the destruction of the enemy's army was won by tactics over 2100 years old.

When in 211 B.C. Hannibal's last effort to raise the siege of Capua by the Romans had failed and he saw that he could not attack the Romans in their entrenched positions, he decided to try to lure them away by marching on Rome. " This is the first instance of which we have any record in which a thrust at the enemy's capital has been used as a feint to withdraw him from a compromising position." [156]

This statement would seem to be contradictory to what has been said about Epaminondas and his attempt upon Sparta. Polybius [157] was so struck by the similarity of the moves that he digresses from his story long enough to institute a comparison. There is, however, quite a difference. Epaminondas was capable of taking Sparta and would have succeeded had his plans not been betrayed to the Spartan leader. Rome, unlike Sparta, was amply garrisoned, and, in addition, Hannibal had made no preparation for siege operations and knew he could not take the city. His effort was a pure feint.

After the disaster at Lake Trasimenus in 217 B.C., Quintus Fabius Maximus was put in charge of the Roman arms. It had hitherto been the policy of Roman generals to attack, to take the initiative on every possible occasion. Fabius clearly saw the need of caution. He dogged Hannibal's line of march, but kept to the hilly country to render the Numidian cavalry useless. He cut off foraging parties and interfered with his adversary's movements in every way compatible with safety. He could not be lured or provoked to battle, but wherever Hannibal went, he followed so that he was nicknamed *paedagogus,* in allusion to the Greek slave who accompanied boys to and from school. Another epithet was *Cunctator,* 'Delayer.'

Small war had been resorted to before this by barbarian tribes, but the Romans were the first powerful nation to develop it into a science. We still pay tribute to the innovator when we speak of Fabian tactics.

Marcellus, 'the sword of Rome,' as Fabius was its 'shield,' did a novel thing for a Roman commander when Hannibal made his second attempt upon Nola (215 B.C.). He armed the citizens of the town and held them in reserve between his own ranks and the walls.[158] Hitherto the *triarii,* men in the third rank, had acted as reserves, but for their own legion. The act of Marcellus is a step toward recognition of the error of systematically and rigidly distributing reserves. The Hannibalic War impressed upon the Romans the necessity of a free or mobile reserve.

Before the first lustrum had elapsed after peace with Carthage, reserves were a matter of course in the Roman army. Polybius [159] uses the battle of Cynocephalae (197 B.C.) as a peg on which to hang the information that in meeting the phalanx the Romans did not extend their front to equal length, but, instead, kept some of their forces in reserve. These reserves were of necessity mobile, since they had to be available to protect either flank from envelopment.

The Roman general of the Second Punic War who learned most from Hannibal was Caius Claudius Nero. This apt pupil used his lessons against his teacher. In 207 B.C., as he was blocking Hannibal at Canusium, he got possession of Hasdrubal's plans to effect a junction with his brother. It was imperative for Rome to frustrate the invader's designs. Nero acted with promptitude. He decided to leave a 'containing' force against Hannibal and to go to the help of Livius in

the North. Keeping Hannibal in the dark as
to his purpose, he marched north with unprecedented speed, using carts and wagons to
hasten his progress, effected a junction with
his colleague, exerted upon Hasdrubal the full
moral effect of his achievement, was the chief
instrument in the destruction of the Carthaginian army at the Metaurus, and returned in
safety to his original position.[160] In two
weeks he had covered some five hundred
miles and gained for Rome the greatest victory of the war. The masterly execution of
the whole operation challenges our admiration.
This campaign finds a place here because it
is the first instance of the effective use of
interior lines. It will always remain a conspicuous illustration of this type of strategy.

Napoleon's offensive-defensive on interior
lines in his campaigns of 1796 and 1814 has
been called a brilliant exposition of the same
principle.[161] In spite of the smaller number
of men engaged and the crude means of transportation that Nero impressed into service to
speed up his line of march, the achievement
is a worthy forerunner of the German shifting
of forces from one front to another during the
Great War.

Of Nero's march Creasy writes as follows: " Viewed only as a military exploit, it remains unparalleled save by Marlborough's bold march from Flanders to the Danube in the campaign of Blenheim, and perhaps also by the Archduke Charles's lateral march in 1796, by which he overwhelmed the French under Jourdain, and then, driving Moreau through the Black Forest and across the Rhine, for a while freed Germany from her invaders."

In the battle of the Metaurus Nero executed a brilliant maneuver. When the Romans were failing to make headway, he detached a force from the right wing, which he was commanding, made a detour of the Roman left flank, and debouched upon the rear of the Carthaginian right. This movement decided the engagement in favor of the Romans.

A similar maneuver makes the battle of Ramillies Marlborough's masterpiece. Jomini [162] tells us that " the real cause of Marlborough's success was his seeing that Villeroi had paralyzed half his army behind Anderkirch and Gette, and his having the good sense to withdraw thirty-eight squadrons from this wing to reinforce his left, which in this

way had twice as many cavalry as the French,
and outflanked them."

At the Trebia Hannibal had had a cavalry
force in ambush upon a flank of the Romans
before battle; Nero combined a front and
flank attack by deployment *after* the battle
had started; "but at Türkheim Turenne
made a still further advance by illustrating
how this principle could be put in practice
by maneuver whilst on the march and before
contact with the enemy." [163]

The battle which Scipio fought in 206 B.C.
near Baecula in Spain against Hasdrubal, son
of Gisgo, is described by Denison [164] as "the
highest development of tactical skill in the
history of Roman arms." We shall, however,
stop only long enough to note that Dodge [165]
finds here another illustration of a threat
against the strategic flank, since Scipio's position endangered Hasdrubal's line of retreat to
Gades.

At Zama in 202 B.C. Scipio gave another
demonstration of tactical ability. Here he
met the great Hannibal at bay.[166] Both
armies were drawn up with cavalry on the
wings. Reversing the situation at Cannae the
Roman cavalry, composed chiefly of Numid-

ians, drove Hannibal's horse from the field.
Returning from the pursuit while the infantrymen were engaged in a terrible struggle, they
fell upon the Carthaginian flanks and rear.
Keeping their banners flying, Hannibal's vet-
'erans fought fiercely with the courage of
despair, but their doom was sealed. The
enemies of Carthage had used Carthaginian
tactics to her undoing.

The leader of the lion's brood was beaten at
last. A life's work was nullified, a life's ambition frustrated, but an ideal of ardent patriotism still remains for the world.

Polybius [167] is unstinted in his praise of
Hannibal and even Livy,[168] a calumniator of
his personal character, cannot refrain from
admiring his great ability. For sixteen years
without active support from home, Hannibal
maintained his army in a hostile country which
had better soldiers than his own. His polyglot
army, consisting of Libyans, Iberians, Ligur-
ians, Celts, Phoenicians, Italians, Greeks, dif-
fering as widely in temperament and customs
as in language, had no bond to hold them
together other than the magnetism of their
leader.

Intensely human, possessed of a sense of

humor, gifted with a fertile imagination, courageous in adversity as in success, an ardent patriot, this great commander calls forth our greatest admiration. I have never heard in a moving-picture theater applause, as spontaneous and as protracted, as that which greeted the flashing on the screen, in D'Annunzio's *Cabiria*, of Hannibal's army surmounting the heights of the snow-clad Alps.

Carthaginian victory would have been a calamity for the Aryan race, yet one reads with sadness Livy's final chapters of Hannibal's career. Had Hannibal's good-fortune been as great as Alexander's, or even commensurate with his own ability, the world would have been his.

With lessons learned in the Second Punic War and under the inspiration of Metaurus and Zama, Roman generalship should have improved, yet it fell back into the more or less traditional methods. This was the character of the reaction inevitable after an unprecedented effort.

The square, which was so common in Greek tactics, was employed by Crassus in his fear of the Parthian cavalry. We are told by

Plutarch [169] that he drew up his men in a deep square with twelve cohorts on each side.

The battle of Carrhae is, however, more remarkable for other aspects of warfare. In 53 B.C. vain-glorious Publius Crassus endeavored to lead an army across the Mesopotamian desert to attack the redoubtable Parthians. When the Romans were in a sea of sand, where there were no natural features to make strategic dispositions possible, the Parthians suddenly attacked. Realizing the helplessness of their infantry against Romans, they had concentrated on cavalry. With their fleet horses and open order they themselves were unassailable, while the serried ranks of their opponents provided easy targets for their long-range bows.

When they were galling the Romans with their fire and threatening to encircle them, the son of Crassus charged them with thirteen hundred horse, five hundred archers and eight cohorts of legionaries. The Parthians fled, but when they had lured their pursuers far out of sight of the rest of the Romans, they turned upon them. Equipped with light, but powerful javelins that outranged the *pilum* and other Roman weapons, they rode round and round the Roman army, showering upon them their missiles so thick and fast that one writer compares them to a hail-storm. Of the detachment of Romans but five hundred survived and they were made prisoners. Under cover of the night, the main body of Romans set out for Carrhae, about thirty miles from the first battle-ground, and finally reached it with difficulty.

The Romans had been outwitted strategically and surpassed tactically. " Here, where the Roman weapons of close combat and the Roman system of concentration yielded for the first time before the weapons of more distant warfare and the system of deploying, was initiated that military revolution which only reached its completion with the introduction of firearms." [170]

The deployed order is seen again in the tactics of Petreius and Afranius, Pompey's lieutenants in Spain. They had been fighting the native tribes of Spain and had adopted in modified form their methods of warfare. They did not keep rank, but fought in loose open order and " did not think it disgraceful to withdraw and yield ground." Caesar's men experienced considerable difficulty on first meeting such tactics.[171] In the American Revolution British regulars at Lexington and Concord, and, in fact throughout the war, seemed helpless against the extended order which took advantage of every natural shelter, a method of warfare that the Colonists had learned in Indian fighting.

When Caesar was thirty-three years old,[172] he lamented that at his age Alexander had conquered the world. The Macedonian had been a student of war from childhood, yet Caesar as a mature man had not even begun his military career. In him were lacking the youthful fire and impetuosity and rashness that characterized Alexander. His late start in war had its influence in making him the purely intellectual type of leader.

That Caesar was not so great a tactician as Alexander and Hannibal and has not left us striking new tactical formations, may be attributed in part to the discipline and matter-of-fact temperament of the Romans. Having better fighting material than either of his predecessors, he probably realized that the familiar methodical distribution of legionaries left less to chance and the personal equation of subordinates.

Naturally he made his plan of battle conform to the character of the ground.[173]   Perhaps his greatest deviation from customary tactics was in a battle with Ariovistus.[174]   He tells us that he opened the battle against the German left wing because he had noticed that that wing was the weakest part of the enemy line.   The implication is that his own left flank was 'refused' and weak.   In fact it with difficulty held out until Caesar could send it help after beating the enemy in front of him.

The great Condé, who was an enthusiastic student of Caesar's *Commentaries,* admired especially the clever manner in which Caesar out-maneuvered Petreius and Afranius in Spain and forced them to surrender without a battle.[175]

At the battle of Pharsalia [176] Caesar stationed himself on the right wing intending to fight in his favorite tenth legion.   Pompey's cavalry concentrated opposite this wing, planning to attack it from the flank and rear, fully confident that no legionaries could stand up against them.   To meet this threat, Caesar secretly withdrew six cohorts from his third line and hid them in the rear in reserve.

When the infantry joined battle, Pompey's proud cavalry began to extend their companies with the intention of enclosing Caesar's right. Thereupon the reserve cohorts sprang forward, and using their spears, not for throwing, but for thrusting at the eyes and face of the horsemen, they drove them shamefully from the field. (These were *Roman* horsemen.) Thereupon the cohorts continued their advance and turned the opposing wing of the enemy.

Gilbert thus sums up Caesar's contribution to military science in this battle: " Caesar here proved the advantage of keeping the third line or reserve concentrated, and not spread out over the whole length of the line of battle, as had hitherto been the Roman practice.[177] He moreover retained the reserve under his immediate personal command. It was posted first in rear of his centre, then moved to the threatened flank, and finally employed to confirm the victory. Caesar had solved the difficult problem of how to sustain the shock of a frontal attack, and at the same time repulse a cavalry attack on flanks or rear." The attack upon the flank, when skilfully executed

by a larger force, had been uniformly successful since the days of Hannibal.

Napoleon says in one of his maxims: "The
distances permitted between corps of an army
upon the march must be governed by the lo-
calities, by circumstances, and by the object
in view." This maxim might well have been
framed from Caesar's procedure.[178] The
student of the Gallic War recalls how the
Nervii were informed that after each of Caesar's legions there was a vast amount of baggage, and that it would not be any trouble
when the first legion had come into camp to
attack it while the others were a great distance
off. The Nervii, however, met with a surprise, for Caesar changed the order and sent
six legions in advance "because he was near-
ing the enemy."

To illustrate Caesar's strategy, we may, as
in the case of Alexander, call attention to a
ruse of his in effecting the passage of a river
in the face of opposition.[179] In 52 B.C. he
wished to cross the Elaver (now Allier).
Upon the other side was Vercingetorix who
had broken down the bridges.

One morning Caesar concealed two legions

in a forest and ordered the remaining four to march up the river with the formation of six. Upon the other side, Vercingetorix kept parallel with the Romans. When he had gone a considerable distance, Caesar set to work to repair a bridge of which the piles had not been entirely destroyed. He led his two legions across without molestation and then summoned the rest of his forces.

"A similar stratagem was successfully employed in 1915. The German and Austrian commanders wished to cross the Vistula in Poland at a point northwest of Ivangorod. They moved their forces upstream in such a way as to lead the Russians to believe that they intended to force a crossing at some distance northeast of the city. At the point previously determined upon, material for pontoon bridges was brought to the bank of the river loaded on wagons which were covered with straw, so that they were reported by the Russian aviators merely as loads of straw; since the Russian commander had no information to the contrary, slight attention was paid to them. The ruse made it possible for the pontooners to start building the bridges before their presence or purpose was suspected.

When the Russians finally brought their artillery to bear at the threatened point, it was too late to check the work; the Teutonic forces completed four bridges over the river and marched across." [180]

Appreciating the importance of speed in military operations, Caesar kept trained engineers in his legions. The expedition with which in one day he threw a bridge across the Arar (Saône), a feat that the Helvetii accomplished with the utmost difficulty in twenty days, so impressed his opponents that they at once sent ambassadors to him.[181] There can hardly be any doubt that this was a pontoon bridge, as was the one constructed over the Sequana (Seine) by Labienus.[182]

In speaking of his indebtedness to Caesar, the Duke of Wellington says of his campaigns in India: " I passed over the rivers as he did by means of baskets and boats of wicker work; only I think I improved upon him, constructing them into bridges and always fortifying them, and leaving them guarded to return by them if necessary." The Duke here refers to the Roman method of using wicker baskets filled with stones as a means of mooring the boats constituting the pontoon bridge.[183]

On the Column of Trajan, which preserves for us a pictorial record of the Emperor's Dacian campaigns, there is to be seen a representation of a very fine pontoon bridge. This obviously served its purpose as well as does its modern counterpart.

The bridge which Caesar threw across the Rhine, to the consternation of modern students of Latin as well as of the ancient Germans, was a remarkable engineering feat. Ten days after he had started to collect material, the army was on the other side. A recent United States army pamphlet on fortification says of Caesar's bridge: " It will be noted that the character of construction used by him is extremely similar to that in use at the present day." [184]

There were three outstanding features of Caesar's campaigns: the capture of decisive points at the outset; the use of the entrenched camp as a movable fortress both to aid in victory and to provide an impregnable rallying place; and the discomfiture of the enemy by breaking up his line of communications.[185] His promptness of decision and rapidity of execution were about on a par with Alexander's. *Veni, vidi, vici* will always be a memorial of his ability to think and act quickly.

He never lost a set battle. Napoleon's enemies finally divined his system of bringing to bear upon some important point a large force against a small one; Caesar's foes never could anticipate his plans.

We have noted Condé's admiration for Caesar's generalship in forcing Afranius and Petreius to surrender without a battle. We have seen that Caesar recognized the real province of a general during a battle. No ancient surpassed him in the art of fortifying. No Roman was his equal in strategy. Of his forces Mommsen says: " Perhaps there never was an army which was more perfectly what an army ought to be." With him the military science of a military and militaristic nation had reached flood-tide.

No general ever wrote a better military narrative than did Caesar. His *Commentaries* were intended to be used as notes, but the ancients shrewdly recognized the futility of trying to improve them.

"*With what his valor did enrich his wit,*
His wit set down to make his valor live."

The Romans were the first nation to undertake an elaborate system of road-construction with the idea of securing mobility. With this end in view they made throughout practically their whole empire a network of roads which were so well designed and built that today after the lapse of some 2,000 years portions of them are still serviceable. This system made it possible for Roman armies to swoop down upon their foes with unexpected speed. It has been said that all roads lead to Rome. From a military point of view it was truer that all roads led from Rome.

The Roman word for baggage, *impedimenta*, 'hindrances,' is an indication that the Romans appreciated at its true value the part played by speed and mobility in military operations.[186] Of the ancient generals, certainly, Alexander and Caesar appreciated as fully as do contemporary generals the value of the time factor in warfare. It required modern methods of transportation to exceed the despatch with which they conducted operations.

" The real art of war had ended with Caesar. For its renaissance we are indebted to Gustavus Adolphus." [187] So highly developed was the Greek and Roman art of war that, once it was lost, it took centuries to restore it to its former position. Without the invention of gunpowder and high explosives, how much farther could modern soldiers have carried the art?

XII. ROMAN CAVALRY

ONE cannot speak with enthusiasm about the cavalry achievements of the Romans. They themselves never became wonderful horsemen. Like the Greeks, they first put men upon horses to accelerate their movements. Their first horsemen were called *celeres*, 'quickmen.' The early *equites* were accompanied by squires who likewise dismounted during the fighting, a situation paralleled in the early history of Greek cavalry.

A step forward in the evolution of Roman cavalry occurred when mounted footmen were assigned genuine cavalry duties. At a critical time in a fight between Romans and Volscians, for instance,[188] a Roman exclaims to the horsemen: "Show to Romans and Volscians that no cavalry are equal to you as cavalry and no infantry as infantry." Even among barbarians the same course of development was followed. The Iberians after conquering horsemen opposed to them would leap to the ground and fight on foot.[189] As

late as the battle of Cannae we find a detachment of Roman cavalry dismounting and
fighting on foot, when the consul Paulus no
longer had strength to control his horse.[190]

At the beginning of the Second Punic War
reconnoitering was already a well recognized
duty of Roman cavalry. When in 218 the
consul Publius Cornelius was on his way to
Spain hoping to obstruct Hannibal's army, he
learned that his opponent was planning the
passage of the Rhone. To get accurate information, he sent a force of three hundred
cavalrymen up the Rhone to make a reconnais-
sance. They fell in with a body of five hundred Numidian horsemen sent out for a similar
purpose. After a clash, fierce out of all proportion to the number of combatants, they
retired victoriously, carrying with them an
omen of victory for the entire war.[191]

The Romans had their first object-lesson
in the handling of cavalry at the battle of the
Trebia late in 218 B.C.[192] In this engagement
Carthaginian cavalry forced the retreat of the
Roman horsemen upon the wings. This
allowed attacks to be made upon the flanks
of the Romans, but still they maintained an
obstinate and successful resistance until an

ambuscade of Numidian horsemen charged the rear of the Roman center. Hannibal owed his victory here to his numerous and well-led cavalry. He was destined to continue to make the most of this branch of the service.

The best demonstration of Hannibal's theory of cavalry tactics was at Cannae.[193] It was the defeat and flight of the Roman cavalry on the right which paved the way for this colossal disaster to Roman arms. In the dispositions for the battle Hannibal placed Numidian cavalry on his right wing facing the cavalry of the Roman allies; on his left he stationed his Gallic and Spanish horse to oppose the Roman horse. Hannibal's horsemen on his left drove the Roman horse from the field and then crossed over in the rear of the Roman lines to aid their own right wing. After overwhelming the Roman squadrons opposed to them, they assailed the Roman legionaries from the rear. Gilbert [194] says of this operation: " The same maneuver was successfully carried out in a precisely similar manner by Condé at the battle of Rocroy, and partially by Cromwell at Naseby."

Of these maneuvers of Hannibal a cavalry critic writes: " His extraordinary skill displayed in the distribution of his cavalry, by which he opposed 8,000 to 2,400, and held back his Numidians on the right until they were assisted by the victorious horse from the other wing is beyond all praise, and proves how thoroughly he appreciated one of the best established principles of modern warfare, that of opposing masses of your own army to fractions of the enemy." [195]

After Cannae Hannibal continued to seek to lure the Romans into engagements in the open where he could maneuver, but the Romans had learned their lessons and with equal assiduity kept to the hilly country. With great discernment Polybius [196] remarks: " I think the reason of the strategy adopted by the two sides respectively was that they both had seen that Hannibal's cavalry was the main cause of the Carthaginian victory and Roman defeat."

The Romans gradually mastered Hannibal's lesson in cavalry tactics, and, strange to say, put an end to the war by a victory which was decided by the tactical action of horsemen. When African allied cavalry under Masinissa attacked the Carthaginians in flank and rear, the cavalry arm of the Roman army had reached its highest efficiency and value.

Of Masinissa who, prior to his defection from the Carthaginians, had ravaged the towns and fields of the Romans in Spain and had brought aid to allies, Dodge [197] writes: " The work of this cavalry-general affords one of the most interesting examples of the proper use of cavalry on a large scale in the history of war."

Of the battle of Carrhae, which has been referred to previously, Denison [198] writes: " The history of war does not show a more brilliant illustration of the cavalry service, nor any instance where so great a result was due solely to the unaided efforts of horsemen. It is remarkable how thoroughly the Parthians appreciated the true value and real use of the horse for military purposes, and how skilfully they utilized two great advantages in war, namely, superior speed in movement, and superior range of missile weapons. These two points, well understood, and ably handled, should always secure success."

The Romans did not, then, handle cavalry skilfully or with imagination. At the battle of Pharsalia, Pompey's cavalry, greatly out-numbering Caesar's as it did, should have carried the day, but it was badly organized and poorly commanded and made a disgrace-ful showing. Even Caesar himself never em-ployed horse in a way comparable to the mag-nificent use of cavalry made by Alexander and Hannibal. This, however, may be more to his credit than otherwise, since he probably recog-nized the limited possibilities of Roman horsemen.

As a rule, after the Second Punic War the Romans were content to entrust the cavalry branch of the service to allies. In his cam-paigns in Gaul Caesar relied on Gallic horse with a small admixture of German, Spanish and Numidian auxiliaries. For a long period afterwards the Gauls furnished a great part of the cavalry.

Of these auxiliaries the Numidians were the most efficient. To them we find the adjective " bridleless " applied several times. The ad-jective is not used figuratively. In describing the cavalry engagement at the Ticinus (219 B.C.), Polybius [199] says that Hannibal put on his front the cavalry " that rode with bridles," while on either flank he placed the Numidians.

The very expression, " that rode with bridles,"
shows that there were some horsemen, obviously the Numidians, who did not use them.

" It is a curious circumstance in this connection that General Hood, of the army of the
late Confederate States of America, has always maintained that if the reins of the cavalry could be cut at the moment of the charge,
the horses would break down the opposition
of any infantry, and that the charge would
always be successful." [200]   He believed that
there was a tendency of the riders to pull up
at the moment of impact and thus to check
the impetuosity of the horses.

Caesar [201] tells us that German cavalry were
accompanied into battle by footmen who were
so agile and swift that they could support
themselves by catching hold of the manes of
the horses and so equal their speed.   In his
war with Rome the Macedonian king, Perseus,
had from his allies, the Basternae, ten thousand horsemen with ten thousand men trained
to run at their sides.[202]   In a charge of the
Scots Greys at St. Quentin in 1914, Highland-
ers accompanied the horsemen and managed
to keep up with them.[203]

It is remarkable how the enemies of Rome

[147]

in different parts of the world recognized at about the same time the irresistible superiority of the legion and began to resort to cavalry and long-distance weapons to fight it. The Armenians, when Lucullus was conducting a campaign against them in 68 B.C., would not allow their infantry to be involved in a conflict, but used their cavalry, and especially their mounted archers, to skirmish with the invaders.[204] Cassivellaunus in Britain saw that nothing could avail against Caesar's infantry and so dismissed the greater part of his forces, keeping 4,000 chariots to harass the line of march.[205] After the Gauls had fought Caesar for several years, Vercingetorix advised them to use the cavalry to devastate the surrounding country, to cut off foraging parties, and to hinder the Romans at every turn.[206] Nowhere, however, were cavalry tactics so successful as at Carrhae.

During the latter days of the Empire, as Rome's enemies, especially on the borders, began to resort more and more to the use of cavalry, the Romans were forced to do likewise. Oman, *A History of the Art of War, The Middle Ages,* puts the last days of the Roman legion at 235–450 and the commencement of the supremacy of cavalry at 450–552. At the battle of Daras against the Persians in 530 A.D. the dispositions of the Roman force under Belisarius were such as to put the brunt of the fighting upon the cavalry.

XIII. ANCIENT AND MODERN ANALOGIES

THE Greeks were a military people, but were never militaristic with the exception of the Macedonian period. The Romans were always militaristic and upon militarism Rome depended as much as did modern Germany for the extension and control of her boundaries. Prior to the Great War we all thought of military Germany as comparable to the Romans, for upon her seemed to have descended the military spirit with many of its attendant qualities.

Neither nation invented the great weapons which it used with greatest effect, but both transformed and transfused those of other nations with their own adaptive and assimilative originality. If we disregard the Zeppelin, which fell far short of expectations, and the long-range gun, used for moral effect, we discover the trend of the inventive skill of the Germans. They did not have the magic genius to invent the submarine, but carried its development farther than did any other nation; they did not invent the airplane, but constructed new models with great success; they did not invent the machine gun, but the outbreak of the war found them equipped with a greater number of such weapons than any other nation and with a greater realization of their value; they were not the first to make gas, but were the first to employ the poison gas wave; even their most effective weapon, the big siege gun, was but a super-howitzer. In tactics, modifications and improvements were made as experience dictated, but they waged the war without a great deal of imagination.

The same sort of originality is seen among the Romans. Even the *pilum*, ' spear,' which they thought of as being as purely Roman as was satire, was simply a super-javelin with modifications and improvements suggested by the weapons of other nations as well as by their own experience. The sword which conquered the world is said to have been of Iberian type. Even their defensive equipment was patterned after foreign models. From the Greeks they learned the art of constructing and operating siege machines. Their legion

was a development of the Doric phalanx
which worked its way up from Magna Graecia.
Hannibal taught them tactics and strategy.
The poet Ovid says: "It is meet to be taught
even by an enemy." We have many acknowledgments, both specific and general, of Roman
indebtedness for arms and equipment.

Modern armies have returned to a number
of accoutrements and devices employed by
the ancients. Military atavism, so to speak,
is seen nowhere more clearly than in the return to armor for the body. In the Great
War helmets proved serviceable against shrap-
nel shells breaking overhead. Cuirasses,
which had apparently been discarded forever,
were again resorted to. Even greaves were
used by Italian barbed-wire cutters and metal
shields were not unknown among French
grenadiers. The title of a recent book, *Helmets and Body Armor in Modern Warfare*,[207]
shows how persistently we revert to ancient
ideas.

A tribute to ancient methods of warfare is
seen in the advent of the tank. Ancient
counterparts of this contrivance are found in
the sheds or mantlets and towers mounted on
wheels, and even on Assyrian reliefs.[207a] As

is the case with the tank they were of different sizes and types of construction. Some of them were designed to protect besiegers approaching a wall, especially for the purpose of filling trenches, sapping, or for undermining fortifications. Others were intended to shelter men operating a ram. Against Massilia 'tortoises'[208] or sheds 60 feet long were employed.

A certain Hegetor of Byzantium constructed a 'tortoise' the base of which was 42 feet by 63 feet. It was moved by eight wheels the height of which was six feet, nine inches. In it was suspended a ram 180 feet long which could be elevated to a height sufficient to throw down a wall 100 feet high.[209]

Still other machines were so high that they could command the tops of walls and at the same time attack the base with rams below. The largest moving tower, 'city-taker,' as the Greeks called such a device, which Demetrius brought against the Rhodians in 305 B.C., is described by Plutarch.[210] "Its base was square, and each of its sides measured at the bottom forty-eight cubits. It rose to a height of sixty-six cubits, and tapered from base to summit. Within, it was divided off into many storeys and chambers, and the side of it which faced the enemy had windows opening out of every storey, and out through these issued missiles of every sort; for it was full of men who fought in every style of fighting. Moreover, it did not totter or lean when it moved, but remained firm and erect on its base, advancing evenly with much noise and great impetus, and this astounded the minds and at the same time greatly charmed the eyes of those who beheld it." [211]

Another writer [212] says that this tower was but little short of being 100 cubits high, that it had eight huge wheels under it, and that it required 3,400 of the strongest men in the army to move it. The 'city-taker' that Demetrius used against Thebes was so big and heavy that in two months it was advanced barely two furlongs.[213]

A Greek whose works were consulted by Vitruvius informs us that the smallest tower should be 60 cubits high with 10 stories, and the largest 120 cubits with 20 stories.[214] For the siege of Jotapata Vespasian ordered three towers 50 feet high to be erected,[215] while at Jerusalem Titus arranged for the construction of three 50 cubits high.[216]

The approach of a moving tower, surmounting the topmost walls, was as terrifying as the attack of an aëroplane and the defense was almost as hopeless.[217] Once it reached fortifications, soldiers in the upper stories could drive off defenders and lower a bridge to the walls. When from the walls of their stronghold the Aduatuci saw Caesar's men constructing such a tower at a distance, they began to jeer at them and to ask how men so small expected to move forward so ponderous a machine. On seeing it approach they were panic-stricken and sent ambassadors to beg for peace, saying that they did not believe that without the help of the gods the Romans could move such a machine at such a pace.[218] "What resource is there," says Vegetius,[219] "when those who were putting their entire hope in the height of the wall suddenly see a battlement of the enemy above them? " This was in reality an attack from the air.

There were still other methods of attacking from above. Against Massilia in the Civil War there was erected a rampart 80 feet high.[220] At Uxellodunum upon a mound 60 feet high was built a tower of ten stories.[221]

Even the conquest of the air does not seem

to have been beyond the imagination of the ancients. Disregarding the story of Daedalus and Icarus, we hear of a wooden machine, called the 'Dove,' which by a system of springs and balances and other contrivances could be made to fly a limited distance. It was the invention of a Pythagorean philosopher named Archytas.[222]

Even the problem of making 'listening devices' was tackled by the ancients. A brazen shield placed upon a wall would indicate by audible vibrations where a tunnel was being dug beneath it.[223]

In 189 B.C. the Romans under Marcus Fulvius Nobilior were besieging Ambracia in Epirus. Under shelter of a covered wall or stoa about 200 feet long, which they constructed parallel to the town fortifications, the Romans started to mine and tunnel. When the height of the excavated material finally betrayed their operations, the besieged set to work to dig a trench parallel to the Roman protection. In order to locate the approaching tunnels, they placed at intervals in the trench a number of very thin brazen vessels. Since these were " extraordinarily sensitive and vibrated to the sound outside," the be-

sieged were able to dig counter-tunnels so ac-
curately that they hit those of the enemy.[224]

This siege gives us also an interesting prototype of a modern gas attack. When the defenders had located the tunnels of the Romans
and made counter-mines, they resorted to the
following device: [225] " Putting in front of them
an earthenware jar, made to the width of the
mine, they bored a hole in its bottom, and,
inserting an iron funnel of the same length
as the depth of the vessel, they filled the jar
itself with fine feathers, and putting a little
fire in it close to the mouth of the jar, they
clapped on an iron lid pierced full of holes.
They carried this without accident to the
mine with its mouth towards the enemy. When
they got near the besiegers they stopped up
the space all around the rim of the jar, leaving only two holes on each side through which
they thrust spears to prevent the enemy coming near the jar. They then took a pair of
bellows such as blacksmiths use, and, having
attached them to the orifice of the funnel, they
vigorously blew up the fire placed on the
feathers near the mouth of the jar, continually
withdrawing the funnel in proportion as the
feathers became ignited lower down. The

plan was successfully executed; the volume of smoke created was very great, and, from the peculiar nature of feathers, exceedingly pungent, and was all carried into the faces of the enemy. The Romans, therefore, found themselves in a very distressing and embarrassing position, as they could neither stop nor endure the smoke in the mines." [226]

There is an ancient analogy even to the tear-gas attack, which places the enemy temporarily *hors de combat*. On one occasion Sertorius was defied by a Spanish tribe, the Charactani, who dwelt in caves on an impregnable cliff. Now it happened that the region abounded in a loose clayey soil. Of this the soldiers made a big pile. The next day the wind blew against the mouths of the caves, and the soldiers stirred up the dust and even drove horses to and fro in it. They repeated the process until the cave dwellers were temporarily blinded and surrendered. [227]

The smoke-screen, which played such a prominent part in naval warfare during the Great War, is not without its ancient analogy. When the Bellovaci and Caesar were encamped close together on one occasion, the Gauls wished to deceive Caesar as to their intentions. Accordingly they set fire to brush and other inflammable material. As Caesar was unable to see through the smoke and feared an ambuscade in case he should advance quickly, the main body of the enemy managed to get a good start before he was sure of their purpose.[228]

In the Peloponnesian War the Spartans brought up fire-throwing engines against the Athenians fortified in Lecythus.[229] References to such contrivances are not infrequent.[230] They remind one of the *Flammenwerfer* of the Great War.

In a modest way the ancients had even a meteorological bureau. They did the best their limited means permitted. They studied the moon, the sun, the clouds and air for indications of the weather and we find Vegetius [231] stressing the importance of noting the actions of birds and fishes for weather forecasts.

But in other ways the actions of birds were found to be much more reliable. Scouts detected the presence of the enemy by noting the alarm manifested by birds frightened from their retreat.[232] This method was practised on the western front in the Great War before it developed into a stalemate. In commenting on the battle of Chancellorsville, Steele [233] writes: " The lines started through the wilderness. The first warning the Eleventh Corps received was not given by its outposts, for they hardly reached the main position ahead of the Confederates; it was given by the deer and rabbits and wild-turkeys of the forest, put to flight by the advance of the enemy."

The use of homing pigeons for military purposes was not unknown to the ancients. In 43 B.C., Decimus Brutus, who was besieged at Mutina by Antony, sent pigeons with messages to the consuls who had approached to relieve him. [234]

It is easy to see that it was not for lack of imagination that warfare was less complex in antiquity than it is today, but rather for want of industries. The imagination of the ancients often inspired on a small scale things that were impossible on a large scale prior to the industrialization of war. [235]

Hitherto we have been concerned chiefly with concrete analogies. Naturally parallels exist with regard to the mental outlook and attitude of the ancients toward war and things military.

In discussing the critical days of the World War during the summer of 1918, Ludendorff, the power behind the German army at that time, thus expresses himself in *The Atlantic Monthly:* [236] " The German troops were not lacking in bravery, nor in tenacity. But, to be successful, they needed something which the leader had no influence on, but with which he cannot dispense, good luck. More than once fortune smiled upon me; but in the decisive moment of the war it left me alone and favored the enemy."

This is an old old cry. Polybius [237] indulges in similar reflections: " It is quite the way of Fortune to confound human calculations by surprises; and when she has helped a man for a time, and caused her balance to incline in his favor, to turn round upon him as though she repented, throw her weight into the opposite scale, and mar all his successes."

Plutarch too comments in the same vein, especially in his *Life of Nicias,* who is a conspicuous example of the mutability of Fortune. Readers who have trudged through Cicero's oration on the Manilian Law will recall that *felicitas,* ' good luck,' is one of the orator's four cardinal requisites for a general.

In his *Great Captains,* Dodge notes the part played by Fortune in the careers of the three greatest generals of antiquity.[238]

National emblems were as much objects of reverence as they are today. Augustus was extremely proud of his achievement in forcing the Parthians to restore the standards of three Roman armies which they had defeated. The recovery of the standards lost to the Germans under Arminius at the battle of Teutoberg Forest in 9 A.D. was a subject for national jubilation. In the Treaty of Versailles the French stipulated that the Germans should return the flags captured in 1870.

For extended comparisons between ancient and modern situations, it must suffice at this point merely to quote two titles, namely: *Our Great War and the Great War of the Ancient Greeks,*[239] by Gilbert Murray, and *Pan-Germanism in the Age of Pericles,*[240] by W. J. Battle.

The basic human passions and impulses were the same in antiquity as they are today. It is the essential oneness of the human race that makes so vital and instructive the experiences of the gifted peoples of antiquity.

XIV. NAVAL INDEBTEDNESS

COULD some feat of magic re-create an ancient fleet, fully equipped and fully manned, to be sent against a single modern battleship, that ancient fleet would have as much chance as a school of minnows against a whale, yet on the sea too the influence of antiquity still spans the centuries.

" That comparatively small sheet of water, the Mediterranean, served as the cradle for sea-power. Those principles of naval warfare, the adherence to or the disobedience of which has resulted in victory or defeat of nations, and has determined the mastery of the world for certain periods, were first demonstrated upon this inland sea." So writes a naval critic.[241]

Lessons are still being drawn from dramas enacted in this restricted body of water. The mere title of a work by Sir Reginald Custance, *War at Sea, Modern Theory and Ancient Practice,* which appeared in the year following the Great War, is a glowing tribute to the ancients.

In E. K. Rawson's *Twenty Famous Naval Battles, Salamis to Santiago,* two ancient engagements by sea are described, Salamis, 480 B.C., and Actium, 31 B.C. Not until sixteen centuries later was there another decisive one, namely, Lepanto in 1571 between the Turks and Don Juan of Austria. Salamis and Actium are included among the fourteen engagements described in J. R. Hale's *Famous Sea Fights from Salamis to Tsu-Shima.*

Many classical parallels to modern maneuvers likewise attest the alertness and resourcefulness of naval men of antiquity. Even in pre-historic Crete there were prototypes of the island kingdom of Great Britain, thalassocracies which owed their security and their independence to control of the sea. With the loss of their naval power they were unable to maintain their position and their dominion ended.

In historic Greek times the first ships built especially for use in warfare were constructed at Corinth and Samos about 700 B.C. We have a passing reference in Thucydides [242] to the first recorded naval engagement between

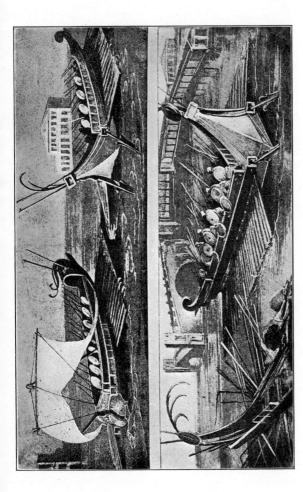

PLATE IV

Naval Tactics (Perhaps a Gladiatorial Combat)
(From a wall-painting in the Temple of Isis, Pompeii)
Reproduced from Schreiber, *Atlas of Classical Antiquities*

Greeks, which was fought by Corinthians and Corcyraeans. Polycrates, a Samian who flourished in the second half of the sixth century B.C., seems to have been the first Greek who was a serious aspirant to sea-power.[243] It was fortunate for the Greeks that they took to the sea before the Persian menace became serious.

War by sea slowly but surely developed into a distinct art. The lengthening of the ships with attendant narrowing of the beam and the introduction of rowers to render the ship independent of the wind are both due to the recognition of the special needs of war by sea.

Data about the dimensions of the trireme, the regular fighting ship of the Greeks, are not available from ancient sources. At Zea, however, a port-town of Athens, there are remains of docks which must have been some one hundred and fifty feet in length and twenty feet in breadth. Presumably the docks are not much larger than the ships they were intended to accommodate. We do not have definite knowledge about the position and arrangement of the rowers and it has even been questioned whether they sat in tiers. Ships have been mentioned with ten, twenty, and

even forty banks of oars, in which it is in-
conceivable that one tier was placed upon
another. Fortunately a knowledge of these
things is not essential for our problem.

A fight at sea was in some measure a re-
production upon floating platforms of a land
engagement. At Salamis there were *epibatai,*
'marines,' who had no nautical duties whatever, but were expected to engage the enemy
in a hand-to-hand encounter when the ships
clashed. We shall see that boarding tactics
as a means of forcing the submission of the
foe were practised by the Romans too and
in fact continued long after the introduction
of cannon on frigates.

As regards battle tactics, the Greeks had
two favorite ways of dealing with a hostile
ship, by sweeping the banks of oars with a
broadside movement and by ramming. The
first method was in purpose and effect exactly
the same expedient as the modern effort to
hit the part of the vessel nearest the engine
room. It put the opponent *hors de combat*
by destroying his motive power.

Ramming was, however, the device employed to destroy a ship. The thing that made
ramming possible as a part of scientific tac-

tics was the emancipation of ships from dependence upon the wind by the introduction of oarsmen. When in more recent times the rough waters of the Atlantic made it imperative to increase the size of ships to such an extent that oars were of no avail, again we see them rendered independent of the wind, this time by the use of steam, and again we find ramming tactics re-introduced in what is virtually a return to the methods of the Greeks and the Romans.

In the Civil War ramming proved effective in the confined spaces of rivers and bays. The Merrimac rammed the Cumberland, but the first fight of steam-driven rams in the history of the world was the battle of Memphis in 1862. Here the Confederates had a fleet of eight rams, while the Union forces had five gunboats and two rams. As late as the Spanish War we had a ram, the Katahdin. It is only the long-range gun that has caused the discarding of the ram. The periscope, however, still makes this method of fighting possible for submarines fighting submarines.

An effective maneuver was the *diekplous*, which consisted of sailing through the enemy's line and attacking him from the stern while he was otherwise engaged. In the battle of Lake Erie, Perry sailed through the British formation in this manner, a maneuver which enabled him to deliver broadsides from both port and starboard.

An outstanding figure in the naval history of all time is the Athenian Themistocles. Though we are inclined to regard Marathon as a decisive battle, he saw that the struggle with the Persian could be terminated successfully only by victory upon the water. Accordingly during the years between Marathon and Salamis he was instrumental in having built and equipped a fleet that not merely saved, but exalted his country. He it was who persuaded the Greeks that ships were meant when the oracle advised them to put their dependence in a "wooden wall." It is not impossible that it was he who inspired the oracle. He was the first European to have a thorough comprehension of the importance of the command of the sea. It is said in fact that in the history of sea-power the name of Themistocles stands without a peer.

The strategy employed by Themistocles may be briefly noted. In the face of strong objections he had the Greek fleet take a position in the strait between Salamis and Attica as the Persians were proceeding southward along the coast of Greece in 480 B.C. This strategic flanking position constituted a menace that the Persians could not disregard. Themistocles precipitated an engagement by giving the Persians the impression that the Greeks were on the point of trying to escape. The *mêlée* took place in the narrow waters where the superior numbers of the Persians availed not and where the superior seamanship and fighting ability of the Greeks were exerted to the best advantage. Darkness finally ended the struggle. The next morning when the Greeks embarked with hearts fortified and encouraged to renew the struggle, they found that the enemy had fled. The Persian threat by sea was past.

In spite of their many ships the Persians had no traditions of success upon the water.[244] Athens had saved herself and Greece through her realization that it takes a sea-power to defeat a nation with a navy, a lesson the truth of which Napoleon was reluctant to admit.

" The battle of Salamis is one of the most instructive battles in the history of the world, in that it proves the overwhelming possibilities of the genius of the strategist; for by nothing else than the genius of Themistocles was the expedition of the Persians brought to naught and Greece saved from ruin." [245]

" The flanking position used by Themistocles . . . to limit the movements of a hostile fleet remains the chief foundation," says Admiral Custance,[246] " on which rests all strategy at sea. For more than three centuries the defence of this country [England] from invasion has been based upon it, the detachments of small ships holding the channel and the narrow seas being covered from an enemy advancing in force out of the Atlantic by the main fleet based on a western port — e.g., Plymouth or Torbay. The same principle might have been applied in the North Sea during the war with Germany, since a fleet in the Forth would have covered the detachments holding the Straits of Dover and the northern exits." According to the same authority,[247] similar strategy to that of Salamis was employed in the Armada Campaign, 1588, and by Togo off Port Arthur, 1904, and in the straits of Tsu-Shima, 1905.

After Salamis the fear of a return of the Persians gave Athens a handle for the formation of the Delian Confederacy. With the

tribute from the confederated states Athens
started the practice of paying her crews,
which at Salamis had consisted of freemen
serving without pay. Higher speed and skill
were developed and the seaman began to feel
a professional pride in handling his ship and
to regard himself as a seaman rather than as
a soldier. He began to maneuver and to realize to the full the possibilities of the prow as
a ram. Here we see the beginning in Europe
of a professional navy.

A half century of development drew very
clearly the line of demarcation between war
by sea and by land. At the very inception of
the Peloponnesian War (431 B.C.–404 B.C.),
Pericles says with emphasis: " Maritime skill
is like skill of other kinds, not a thing to be
cultivated by the way or at chance times; it
is jealous of any other pursuit which distracts
the mind for an instant from itself." [248]

In this great conflict with Sparta the Athenian ships had better prows and greater mobility than formerly, but the narrower beam en-
tailed a reduction in the number of marines.
This was the beginning of the age-long conflict between fighting power and speed.

An advance in tactics was attained in the

same war by the skilful disposition of ships in groups or squadrons and methods by which they were thrown into battle. Naturally flanking movements were carried out on a large scale, but the greatest improvement was seen in the endeavor to bring overpowering forces to bear upon parts of the enemy formation while weaker detachments of the attacking force 'contained' or checked the rest of the enemy.

In the battle of Arginusae, which was fought in 406 B.C. in the northern Aegean, the Spartans and their friends had the longer line and intended to overlap the Athenians. "The Athenian dispositions," says Admiral Custance,[249] "seem designed to hold the centre with a force equal to that of the enemy, while two masses, each of sixty ships, were launched against the thirty ships on either side of the centre; in other words, their aim was to throw the whole fleet of one hundred and fifty ships on to eighty or ninety of the enemy with the view of getting a decision before the ships in the overlap could come into action. The result was a complete defeat of the allies, who lost seventy-seven triremes as against twenty-five lost by the Athenians. If the above view is correct, the tactical skill of the Athenians in the battle was of a high order."

The same writer says that "Arginusae was the prototype of Trafalgar," a statement that should not be construed to mean that Nelson had Arginusae in mind, but that, like the Greeks, he was employing the principle of concentrating the bulk of his fleet upon a fraction of the enemy.

At the battle of Cynossema, 411 B.C., in the Hellespont, new tactics were tried against the Athenians by the commander of the allied fleet under the Lacedaemonians: "The battle illustrates a step in the development of tactics, in that the centre and one wing were held by a frontal attack while an attempt was made to outflank the other wing."[250]   Still other Greek naval battles exemplify this principle of concentration of force.

During the long course of the Peloponnesian War the Syracusans had a fine chance to use to advantage the principles of strategy employed by Themistocles at Salamis.   In June 415 B.C. an Athenian fleet gathered at Corcyra for an attack on Sicily.   The Syracusans were urged by Hermocrates, whom Captain Mahan styles an " untaught genius," to send all their available ships to take up a strategic flanking position at Tarentum, so that they might set upon the Athenians as they rounded the promontory of Iapygia at the heel of Italy. The Syracusans could not, however, be convinced that the Athenian concentration at Corcyra was aimed at them and so lost a golden opportunity.

How permanent the basic principles of naval strategy are and how thoroughly the Greeks had mastered them cannot be better shown than by quoting Captain Mahan,[251] who thus sums up the naval side of the Athenian expedition against Sicily: " This episode in the Peloponnesian War . . . gives us all the conditions of a distant maritime expedition in any age. We have the home base, Athens; the advanced intermediate bases at Corcyra and other points, which played for Athens the part that Gibraltar, Malta, and foreign coaling stations have done and still do for Great Britain; the objective, Syracuse; the neutral, doubtful, or hostile country to be passed, across the Ionian Sea or along the coasts of Italy; the enemy's advanced post in Tarentum and sister cities; the greater naval power in Athens;

the smaller but still respectable fleet of Syracuse; the difficulty of communications; the tactical embarrassment of a train of supply ships; the tactical difficulty of ships deeply laden for a long voyage, which exists in a degree today; the tactical difficulty of the fatigue of rowers, which has disappeared; the wisdom of meeting the enemy half way and harassing his progress; the danger of awaiting him at home on the defensive; the perception of the navy's true sphere, the offensive. All these broad outlines, with many lesser details, are to be found in this Athenian expedition, *and most of them involve principles of present application.* In fact, put this early galley expedition under a microscope and there is (*sic*) seen realized the essential leading features of any maritime invasion."

In Thucydides [252] a significant comment is put into the mouth of Pericles as he advocates the vigorous prosecution of the Peloponnesian War. As he contrasts the position of the Spartans and Athenians he says: "If they attack our country by land, we shall attack theirs by sea; and the devastation, even of part of Peloponnesus, will be a very different thing from that of all Attica. For they, if

they want fresh territory, must take it by
arms, whereas we have abundance of land
both in the islands and on the continent;
such is the power which the empire of the sea
(τὸ τῆς θαλάσσης κράτος) gives." The Greek
words really mean 'sea-power' in all the ful-
ness of meaning with which that term is employed by Captain Mahan and other technical
writers. Thucydides would surely include
under this term "all that tends to make a
people great upon the sea or by the sea." [253]

The writer of the article on *Sea-Power* in
the Encyclopaedia Britannica (1902) thus
pays his respects to Thucydides: "Before
Mahan no historian — not even one of those
who specially devoted themselves to the narra-
tion of naval occurrences — had evinced a
more correct appreciation of the general principles of naval warfare than Thucydides. He
alludes several times to the importance of getting command of the sea. Great Britain would
have been saved some disasters and been less
often in peril had British writers . . . possessed the same grasp of the true principles of
defense as Thucydides did."

The span from the Greek historian to Mahan
is a long, long one. As we shall see later, how-

ever, Thucydides's fellow-countryman, Polybius, was not much inferior in his appreciation of the value of sea-power.

Napoleon quotes an adage to the effect that he who is master of the sea is master of the land. The ancients realized as clearly as the nations engaged in the Great War the difficulty of conducting successful operations on land without control of the sea. Alexander did not feel free to advance into the heart of Persia until he had neutralized the power of the Persian fleet by subduing the coast towns in Asia Minor and Phoenicia. He has been accused of wasting seven months in the siege of Tyre, but Napoleon said that he would have stayed there seven years if necessary. Just before undertaking the siege, Alexander said: " I see that the expedition against Egypt is not safe while the Persians are in command of the sea, nor is it safe to pursue Darius if we leave behind us the city of the Tyrians wavering in her loyalty." [254]

Alexander understood how to combine the actions of land and naval forces. After describing the coöperation of the Japanese fleet and army as they pushed their base northward from Korea in their war against China,

[177]

Baron Von der Goltz continues: " In the ages of antiquity we see the same thing carried out on a large scale by Alexander, who caused his land forces to be accompanied by the fleet of Nearchus, on the march to and from India." [255]

As for the Romans, their sea-power was artificially stimulated, since, like that of the Germans, it was not built upon the maritime character or tradition of the people, but founded upon a clear realization of the relation of sea-power to conquest and world-dominion.

When Antony decided to fight Octavius upon the sea off Actium, a centurion who had suffered many wounds in service thus addressed his commander with tears: " Imperator, why do you distrust these wounds or this sword, and rest your hopes in miserable logs of wood? Let Egyptians and Phoenicians fight on sea, but give us land, on which we are accustomed to stand and to die or to vanquish our enemies." [256] The attitude of the centurion may be regarded as fairly representative. It was cool reasoning that put the Roman navy upon the sea. When emergencies passed, Rome was apt to be indifferent to its navy.

As soon as the Roman octopus began to

reach out its tentacles beyond the confines of Italy, the Romans grasped the significance of sea-power. We find that in 261 B.C., three years after the inception of the First Punic War, the Romans were eager to meet the Carthaginians upon the water, because " so long as the Carthaginians were in undisturbed command of the sea, the balance of success could not incline decisively in their favor." [257]

After this same war had dragged out its weary length for twenty-two years, the Romans in 242 B.C. despatched a fleet to Sicily under the command of Gaius Lutatius Catulus. Of him Polybius says: [258] " He kept in mind the original idea of this expedition, that it was by a victory at sea alone that the result of the whole war could be decided."

Again in the Second Punic War the Romans showed a clear vision as to the value of sea-power. Its advantage was fully manifested when, after Hannibal had eluded Scipio at the Rhone, they were enabled to transport their army to Italy and to face the invader at the Po. The command of the sea finally made it possible for the Romans to carry the war into Africa. By the terms of the ensuing peace Carthage was forced to give up all but ten triremes, a surrender that showed that her conqueror appreciated the meaning of supremacy upon the water as fully as did the vanquishers of Germany in the World War.

In May 49 B.C., during the conflict between Caesar and Pompey, Cicero in a letter to his friend Atticus [259] states that even if Pompey loses the Spains, the contest will not be decided, for Pompey has a fleet and is going to resort to the plan of Themistocles: " For he thinks the man who holds the sea must come off master."

Of the battle off Actium fought in 31 B.C. between Antony and Octavius a naval authority writes: " Actium affords us the spectacle of two experienced generals commanding large armies facing each other, acknowledging the all-importance of sea-power by leaving those armies inactive and taking to the sea and deciding the sovereignty of the then known world with maritime forces far inferior in number to the available land forces impotently standing by as spectators. Actium witnessed the full development of sea-power; its firm establishment as the first and governing principle of warfare occurred in the centuries that followed." [260]

[180]

As regards battle formations, perhaps the most conspicuous example of Roman originality is at the battle of Ecnomus, where they met the Carthaginians in 256 B.C. Two files of ships were arranged in the form of a wedge while a third squadron took position in a single line at the base so that the completed formation resembled a triangle, at the apex of which were the ships of the two consuls. In this formation they bore down upon the enemy. Unwilling to face the impact, the Carthaginian center made a ' strategic retreat.' " This action is celebrated," says Silburn, " and marks a distinct advance in sea-power, as the first example of ' breaking the line.' " [261]

In the naval battle of the Saints, fought between Rodney and De Grasse off San Domingo in 1782, Rodney cut the line of his opponent and " unconsciously repeated the Roman admiral's tactics at Ecnomus." [262]

The Romans, realizing their inferior seamanship, went much farther than the Greeks in reproducing the conditions of war by land. At the battle of Actium the ships of Antony were too heavy to acquire sufficient speed to ram and Caesar's ships were too light to stand an impact upon them. " The battle, therefore, was like land fights," says Plutarch,[263] " or, to speak more exactly, like the assailing of a fortress; for three and four of Caesar's ships at the same time were engaged about one of the ships of Antony and the men fought with light shields and spears and poles and fiery missiles; the soldiers of Antony assailed them also with catapults from wooden towers."

Besides Plutarch, we find that Polybius, Livy, Vegetius and other writers were struck by the resemblance of Roman naval engagements to fights on land. While the Romans did employ naval tactics and even made some additions to what they learned from the Greeks, they realized the limitations of their ships and of their seamanship. In general the tendency of their tactics was to reproduce the conditions obtaining on land. In order to neutralize their hopeless inferiority in seamanship at the battles of Mylae, 260 B.C., and Ecnomus, 256 B.C., in the First Punic War, they equipped their vessels with a ' crow,' a sort of gangway that could be raised and lowered at will. This was fitted with a heavy spike at the elevated end so that when it fell, it not only grappled the two ships, but provided a bridge. Thus we see the ramming tactics of the Greeks superseded by boarding tactics. Such tactics persisted and even in the days of frigates many engagements were terminated only when the ships had been lashed together and victory decided by hand to hand engagements of boarding parties. John Paul Jones said of the fight with the Serapis: " The enemy's bowsprit, however, came over the Bon Homme Richard's poop by the mizzenmast, and I made both ships fast together in that situation."

Plutarch's second comparison of the sea-fight at Actium to a siege operation is by far the more accurate one. The similarity struck Vegetius, too, for he says that men fought from ramparts and towers on ships just as if from walls. Artillery, which was not always employed in field operations, was freely used. Hooks, such as besiegers used to loosen stones in the walls, were employed to catch and cut rigging. The chemical warfare of the defenders of cities was likewise imitated by the use of oil, pitch, bitumen, resin and other highly combustible material. Even with these tactics bridges were still used.[264] Occasionally even the Greeks used clumsy tactics. Thucydides [265] tells us that an engagement between

Corinth and Corcyra in 432 B.C. had " almost the appearance of a battle by land," and he remarks that " brute force and rage made up for the want of tactics."

The towers that were placed in the prows to provide a means of raking the enemy's decks, are lineal ancestors of the forecastles of modern ships which were used originally for the same purpose.

Military-tops were not used on Greek and Roman war-ships, although merchantmen employed them as part of their defense against pirates. Long before the days of the classical nations, Egyptian war-ships had used them and they were to appear again in the Byzantine period.[266]

We have seen that tactics of the ancients have been repeated in succeeding ages and that the principles of strategy which they inaugurated are as fundamental and as far-reaching as those on land. Their achievements on the water are a fitting complement to those on land and will still reward the student of naval history and progress. That the lessons of sea-power have passed unheeded has been ascribed to their being buried under the volume of detail concerning engagements

[1 8 4]

by land. The writings of Captain Mahan have again focused attention upon them.

Every war possesses features of its own by land and sea which differentiate it from all its predecessors, yet in broad outlines warfare even today retains characteristics which have long since been worked out as fundamental.

XV. CONCLUSION

THE principles of warfare through the correct application or disregard of which battles are won or lost on both land and sea were first demonstrated in Europe by the Greeks and Romans. From dramas that were enacted in so small a theater of operations lessons may still be drawn. Writing in 1890 Colonel Dodge [267] says: " War is scarcely more perfect today, according to our resources in arts and mechanics, than it was twenty odd centuries ago among the Greeks according to theirs."

The thoughtful reader, having the Great War in mind, may, perhaps, regret that the Greeks and Romans have made lasting contributions to a science that carries death and destruction in its path. Arts and culture and the sciences in general thrive, however, only in an atmosphere of freedom. Without their martial skill the Greeks would not have had a chance in their day to cultivate their special gifts; without recourse to arms Rome would

CONCLUSION

not, anciently, have been able to spread law
and order and civilization in Western Europe.

The classical nations, it must be noted, are
not the sole peoples that have, unhappily,
used military power to protect their independence and their growth, and then, with the at-
tainment of these objects, diverted that same
power to reduce other nations to a condition
they themselves found intolerable.

Alexander aspired to "sow Greece"[268]
throughout the world. The Germans seized
upon this statement to justify their own
method of spreading *Kultur*. That the Greeks
sowed their civilization more successfully by
the arts of peace than by those of war is one
of the lessons of history that the world is slow
to learn.

Our own nation too might have profited by
lessons that antiquity has to teach. Pericles
said to the Athenians: [269] "To remain at peace
when you should be going to war may often
be very dangerous." If there are degrees of
truth, such a statement was never more true
than during the first two years and a half of
the Great War.

Vegetius is thoroughly Rooseveltian: "No
one," says he,[270] "has the courage to provoke

[187]

or to do injury to that realm or people which he knows to be prepared and disposed to resist and requite."

" We should have scant capital to trade on," says ex-President Wilson, " were we to throw away the wisdom we have inherited and seek our fortunes with the slender stock we ourselves have accumulated."

In this connection I cannot forbear quoting Gilbert [271] once more: " With perhaps the sole exception of such men as Parmenio, Craterus, Ptolemy, Hephaestion, Meleager, Coenus, and others of the Alexandrian galaxy of subordinate commanders, history does not show us a body of officers that had gone through the amount of hard fighting experienced by Ney, Soult, Davout, Victor, Junot, Masséna, and others of Napoleon's marshals. This experience was spread over a period of twenty years, and was gained under the most varied conditions. Yet it is a remarkable fact that without exception they one and all failed to justify the trust imposed in them when in independent command and left in a great measure to their own resources and initiative, and that one of them, by no means the least famous [Ney], we find charged with stupidity.

Their chief, on the other hand, is a standing example of the result of the fruits of study applied in this field."

Advances in civilization are effected by building upon the heritage of the past. The ancient treasures of experience and wisdom will always be a source of enrichment for those sufficiently enlightened to use them. The art of war is only one of the many arts and fundamental branches of human endeavor whose recorded history begins with a résumé of the contributions of the ancients. It too illustrates the continuity of human progress.

It has been well said that the roots of the present lie deep in the past and that he who would know the present must study the past. We think what we think and do what we do and are what we are largely because of what the Greeks and Romans thought and did and were. The military and naval history of these ancient nations, which lies at the foundation of European experience, must be part of our knowledge if we are to apprehend our own instincts truly, if we are to avert inherent evils and above all create a more enlightened future.

NOTES AND BIBLIOGRAPHY

NOTES

1. Polybius, I. 1; E. S. Shuckburgh, *The Histories of Polybius*, Translated, 2 vols., London, 1889. I have used Shuckburgh's translation for all quotations from Polybius.

2. See J. A. Breasted, *The Battle of Kadesh*, Chicago, 1904.

3. *Cyropaedia*, VI. 3. 24. The translation is that of H. G. Dakyns, *The Works of Xenophon*, 4 vols., London, 1890, *seq.*

3a. Delbrück, *Die Strategie des Perikles, erläutert durch die Strategie Friedrichs des Grossen*, Berlin, 1890. Compare also the title of another work by Delbrück, *Die Perserkriege und Burgunderkriege*, Berlin, 1887.

4. Rear-Admiral Bradley A. Fiske, *The Art of Fighting*, p. 312.

5. *Demetrius*, 44.

6. *Moralia*, 326–327.

7. Hogarth, in *The Journal of Philology*, XVII. 22 (1888).

8. Thuc., II. 39. The translation is that of H. Dale, London, 1856.

9. XI. 14.

10. XXXV. 28.

11. XLII. 47.

12. Livy, XXI. 54.

13. Dodge, *Caesar*, p. 643.

14. *American Campaigns*, Washington, D. C., 1909; I. 146.

15. II. 3; Translation, Perrin, in *The Loeb Classical Library*, New York, 1917.

16. Aelianus, *De Instruendis Aciebus*, 8.

17. XVIII. 29.

18. Polyb., XVIII. 26.

19. Caes., *B. G.*, I. 25.

20. For an extended comparison of the phalanx and the legion, see Polybius, XVIII. 28–32.

21. Thuc., III. 94.

22. Thuc., III. 98.

23. Thuc., IV. 32–36.

24. Xen., *Hell.*, IV. 5. 13 *seq.*

25. Botsford, *A History of Greece*, New York, 1905, p. 242.

26. See George Grote, *A History of Greece*, London, 1851–56; XII. 73.

27. Grote, *op. cit.*, XII. 89–90.

28. The "Leuctrian wedge" was somewhat different, being formed by the "refusing" of the entire line in sections. It is hardly probable that there was a phalangite serving as the apex of a body of men.

29. G. F. R. Henderson, *Stonewall Jackson*, New York, 1898; I. 199.

30. See E. Norman Gardiner, *Greek Athletic Sports and Festivals*, London, 1910, p. 346.

31. Diod. Sic., XII. 28.

32. *Ibid.*, XX. 95.

33. Appian, VIII. 98.

34. XIV. 42. 1.

35. In Vegetius, II. 25, however, *onagri* are referred to as shooting arrows also. Lydus, *De Mag.*, I. 46, speaks of a vulgar use of the word *onager* in the sense of catapult.

36. Sir R. Payne-Gallwey, *The Projectile-Throwing Engines of the Ancients*, p. 13.

37. III. 7. 23; V. 6. 3.

38. *B. C.*, II. 2.

39. *Hist.*, III. 23.

40. Sir Payne-Gallwey, *op. cit.*, pp. 25 and 23, respectively.

41. Philon, *De Telorum Constructione*, in Thévenot, *Veteres Mathematici*, Paris, 1693, pp. 73–74.

42. *B. G.*, VII. 25, Translation, H. J. Edwards, in *The Loeb Classical Library*, New York, 1917.

NOTES

43. Philon, IV. 78. 33; cf. H. Diels, *Antike Technik,* Leipzig and Berlin, 1920, p. 106.

44. Diod. Sic., XIV. 42. 1.

45. *Ibid.,* XIV. 47. 7.

46. Athenaeus, *De Machinis,* in Thévenot, *op. cit.,* pp. 3-4.

47. Diod. Sic., XVI. 74.

48. Livy, XXVI. 47. 5.

49. Josephus, *The Jewish War,* III. 7. 9.

50. Josephus, *op. cit.,* V. 9. 2.

51. Polyb., XXXVI. 5.

52. Strabo, XVII. 15.

53. Plut., *Sulla,* 12.

54. Plut., *Anton.,* 38.

55. Diod. Sic., XIV. 50. 4.

56. Diod. Sic., XX. 85. 4.

57. Arrian, I. 6.

58. Arrian, IV. 4. 4.

59. Arrian, IV. 29. 7.

60. Polyb., XI. 12.

61. *B. G.,* VIII. 14. 5.

62. *B. C.,* III. 45. 3.

63. Veg., II. 25.

64. Dodge, *Alexander,* p. 87.

65. VI. 112.

66. Thuc., V. 70.

67. This statement may well be taken at its face value. It is said that at the siege of Jotapata by Vespasian the arrows flew so fast that they shut off the light of the sun. (Josephus, *The Jewish War,* III. 7. 27; see also Plin., *Nat. Hist.,* XVI. 159.)

68. Grundy, *The Great Persian War,* p. 553.

69. Thuc., IV. 125.

70. For an instance of much earlier employment of the square by Egyptians, see Xen., *Cyropaedia,* VI. 3.

71. Thuc., VI. 67.

72. *Anab.,* III. 2. 36.

73. Diod. Sic., XVI. 4. 6.

74. Gilbert, *The Evolution of Tactics,* p. 131.

75. Thuc., IV. 125, 127.

76. Thuc., VI. 67.

77. *Anab.*, VI. 5. 9–11.

78. Thuc., II. 66.

79. Thuc., III. 107. For another instance of overlapping, see Thuc., V. 71.

80. Thuc., IV. 96.

81. There was a tendency on the part of the soldiers themselves to shift to the right to prevent their shieldless side from being exposed to the enemy. See Thuc., V. 71.

82. Grundy, *Thucydides and the History of his Age*, p. 271.

83. A. G. Bradley, *The Fight with France for North America*, Westminster, 1900, p. 223.

84. Dodge, *Napoleon*, I. 293.

85. Diod. Sic., XVI. 4. 5.

86. Arrian, I. 2.

87. Grote, *op. cit.*, XII. 308.

88. Livy, XXI. 27. Compare also the feint of Xenoetas at the Tigris, Polyb., V. 46.

89. Diodorus Siculus, XVII. 86. 3, says that Alexander crossed the Indus on a bridge of boats. Arrian, V. 7, is, however, not so sure, but this feeling is probably due to the failure of his authorities to specify the character of the bridge.

90. See Grote, *op. cit.*, V. 24 *seq.*

91. Grundy, *The Great Persian War*, p. 552.

92. Thuc., V. 57.

93. Arrian, I. 6.

94. Herod., IX. 39.

95. Denison, *History of Cavalry*, p. 23.

96. Arrian, III. 12.

97. See Grundy, *Thucydides and the History of his Age*, p. 281.

98. *Op. cit.*, p. 32.

99. Dodge, *Alexander*, p. 661.

100. Denison, p. 33.

101. See Denison, p. 256.

102. Livy, I. 16.

103. Th. Mommsen, *The History of Rome;* I. 90. The translation is that of W. P. Dickson, New York, 1900.

104. Dio Cass., XXXVIII. 40.

105. *T. D.,* II. 16. 37.

106. *Op. cit.,* III. 5. 1.

107. *Inst.,* X. 1. 114.

108. Plut., *Caes.,* 3.

109. O. Weise, *Language and Character of the Roman People,* p. 48. The translation is that of Strong and Campbell, London, 1909.

110. Weise, *op. cit.,* p. 43.

111. IX. 3.

112. F. Marx, *C. Lucilii Carmina,* Leipzig, 1904; I. 42; cf. Livy, IX. 18.

113. Aen., VI. 847 ff., Translation by Th. C. Williams, Boston and New York, 1908.

114. I. 1.

115. Veg., I. 5. 6.

116. *Ibid.,* I. 7.

117. *Ibid.,* I. 11.

118. *Ibid.,* I. 12.

119. *Ibid.,* I. 14.

120. *Ibid.,* II. 23.

121. *Loc. cit.*

122. *Loc. cit.*

123. This reminds one of the statement in Plutarch, *Lycurgus,* 22, that the Spartans were the only men in the world to whom war brought a respite in the training for war.

124. Veg., III. 2.

125. Caes., *B. G.,* II. 20.

126. *Ibid., B. C.,* III. 93.

127. VIII. 8. 2.

128. London, 1903, p. 260.

129. Veg., I. 24.

130. *B. C.,* III. 63.

131. Veg., III. 8.

132. See T. Rice Holmes, *Caesar's Conquest of Gaul,* p. xxx.

133. Plut., *Crassus*, 10.

134. *B. G.*, VII. 69–89.

135. It has been suggested that the soldiers were comparing the *cippi* to gravestones.

136. *B. C.*, III. 47.

137. *Caesar*, p. 518.

138. *Pamphlet on the Evolution of the Art of Fortification*, p. 33.

139. XVIII. 18.

140. Vitruvius, X. 16. 11, Translation, M. H. Morgan, Cambridge, Mass., 1914.

141. Livy, V. 38.

142. A. P. F. von Tirpitz, *My Memoirs*, New York, 1919; II. 161. The reader will doubtless recall this story which is told in Livy's most delightful vein. Alban and Roman armies had agreed to settle the question of supremacy by the outcome of a battle between champions. As it chanced, each army had a family of three brothers who were triplets, the Curiatii (Albans) and Horatii (Romans). These were selected to represent their nations. At the first encounter of these youths, two Horatii fell, while all the Albans were wounded. The surviving Horatius took to flight, but when the injured Albans became separated in the pursuit, he turned and vanquished them one at a time.

143. Polyb., I. 40.

144. Polyb., III. 42–43; Livy, XXI. 27.

145. XXI. 44.

146. *Hannibal*, p. 258.

147. *The Evolution of Tactics*, p. 18.

148. *Hannibal*, p. 292.

149. See Polyb., III. 113–117; Livy, XXII. 45–50.

150. Dodge, *Hannibal*, p. 652.

151. Wm. L. McPherson, *The Strategy of the Great War*, New York, 1920, p. 88.

152. The younger Moltke made changes in Von Schlieffen's plan, notably in greatly strengthening the left wing, but the idea of a great strategic turning movement through Belgium was Von Schlieffen's.

153. A diagram of the German conception of ideal battle tactics, based on Cannae, can be found in *The Times History of the War*, London, I. 247 (1914).

154. The encircling movement was extended by troops and some cavalry brought down from the North from the army in front of another invading Russian force under Rennenkampf.

155. Thomas G. Frothingham, *A Guide to the Military History of the World War, 1914–1918*, Boston, 1920, p. 33.

156. Dodge, *Hannibal*, p. 483.

157. IX. 8–9.

158. Livy, XXIII. 44.

159. XVIII. 32.

160. Livy, XXVII. 43–51.

161. Gilbert, *op. cit.*, p. 19.

162. *The Art of War*, p. 312.

163. Gilbert, p. 54.

164. *A History of Cavalry*, p. 60.

165. *Hannibal*, pp. 566–567.

166. Livy, XXX. 33–35.

167. XI. 19.

168. XXVIII. 12.

169. *Crassus*, 23. Antony too used the hollow square to protect himself from the Parthians. See Plut., *Ant.*, 42. 1.

170. Mommsen, *op. cit.*, V. 158.

171. *B. C.*, I. 43–44.

172. Suet., *Div. Jul.*, 7, and Dio Cassius, XXXVII. 52; but compare Plut., *Caes.*, 11.

173. *E. g., B. G.*, II. 22.

174. *B. G.*, I. 52.

175. *B. C.*, I. 65–66. Cf. J. B. De Bossuet, *Oraison Funèbre de Louis de Bourbon, Prince de Condé*, in *Oraisons Funèbres*, Paris, 1886.

176. *B. C.*, III. 88–95; Plut., *Pomp.*, 68–72.

177. Compare previous comments on reserves.

178. *B. G.*, II. 17.

179. *B. G.*, VII. 35.

180. F. W. Kelsey, *Caesar's Commentaries*, New York, 1918, xv-xvi.

181. *B. G.*, I. 13.

182. *Ibid.*, VII. 58.

183. Caesar certainly employed this method on the Guadalquiver in Spain (*Bell. Hisp.*, 5). Arrian, V. 7, digresses from his story long enough to record Roman ways of construction.

184. Page 28 of the pamphlet prepared under Major General Black (See bibliography).

185. Dodge, *Caesar*, p. 347.

186. We are told that Philip of Macedon made his soldiers carry their own provisions, thus getting rid of a large number of wagons. He also limited the number of servants (Frontinus, *Strat.*, IV. 1. 6).

187. Gilbert, *op. cit.*, p. 34.

188. Livy, IV. 38.

189. Diod. Sic., V. 33.

190. Livy, XXII. 49.

191. Livy, XXI. 29.

192. Polyb., III. 73–74.

193. Polyb., III. 113–117; Livy, XXII. 45–50.

194. *Op. cit.*, p. 37.

195. Denison, *op. cit.*, p. 55.

196. IX. 3.

197. *Hannibal*, p. 560.

198. *Op. cit.*, p. 85.

199. III. 65.

200. Denison, *op. cit.*, p. 58.

201. *B. G.*, I. 48.

202. Plut., *Paul.*, 12. 2.

203. See Kelsey, *op. cit.*, xv, xxv.

204. Plut., *Lucullus*, 31.

205. *B. G.*, V. 19.

206. *B. G.*, VII. 14.

207. By Bashford Dean, New Haven, 1920.

207a. In the British Museum visitors are told that the Assyrian reliefs inspired the idea of a protecting device that could be moved against the enemy. Certainly the

American caterpillar tractor solved the problem of the means of locomotion.

208. Caes., *B. C.*, II. 2. 4; II. 10. 1.

209. Vitruv., X. 15.

210. *Demetrius*, 21.

211. Translation, B. Perrin, in *The Loeb Classical Library*, New York, 1920.

212. Diod. Sic., XX. 91.

213. Plut., *Demetrius*, 40.

214. Vitruvius, X. 13.

215. Josephus, *The Jewish War*, III. 7. 30.

216. *Op. cit.*, V. 7. 1.

217. The defense consisted in setting fire to the towers, digging mines beneath the course they were to take, or erecting counter-towers, methods which were not very frequently successful.

218. *B. G.*, II. 30–31.

219. IV. 17.

220. Caes., *B. C.*, II. 1; cf. *B. G.*, VII. 24.

221. Caes., *B. G.*, VIII. 41.

222. Aul. Gell., *Noct. Att.*, X. 12.

223. Aeneas Tacticus, 37.

224. Polyb., XXI. 28.

225. *Ibid.*

226. In a note to the passage Shuckburgh says: " Smoking out an enemy was one of the regular maneuvres. See Aen. Tact., 37. It was perhaps suggested by the illegal means taken by workmen in the silver mines to annoy a rival; for we find an Athenian law directed against it."

227. Plut., *Sert.*, 17. 1–7.

228. *B. G.*, VIII. 15.

229. Thuc., IV. 115.

230. *E. g.*, Diod. Sic., XX. 96; Plut., *Sulla*, 12. 3.

231. IV. 41.

232. Frontinus, *Strat.*, I. 2. 7–8.

233. *American Campaigns*, I. 341.

234. Plin., *N. H.*, X. 110; cf. Frontinus, *Strat.*, III. 13. 8.

235. An interesting collection of analogies between ancient and modern methods of warfare has been made by Professor F. W. Kelsey, *Caesar's Commentaries,* New York, 1918, ix-xxvii. A number of parallels may be found in two articles written by myself, "The Ancients and the War," in *The Classical Weekly,* XI. 142–144 (1918), and "The Ancients and the War: Addenda," in *The Classical Weekly,* XII. 129–132 (1919).

236. "The American Effort," in *The Atlantic Monthly,* CXXIX. 683 (1922).

237. XXIX. 22.

238. See *Alexander,* pp. 210–212, 275; *Hannibal,* pp. 646–647; *Caesar,* p. 761.

239. New York, 1920.

240. *The Texas Review,* III. 275–296 (1918); IV. 38–51 (1918).

241. P. A. B. Silburn, *The Evolution of Sea-Power,* p. 10.

242. I. 13.

243. Herod., III. 122.

244. Mardonius himself referred to the Persians as "landsmen" (Plut., *Aristides,* 10. 2).

245. Fiske, *The Art of Fighting,* p. 90.

246. *War at Sea,* p. 109.

247. *Ibid.,* p. 27.

248. Thuc., I. 142.

249. Custance, p. 43.

250. *Ibid.,* p. 42.

251. *Naval Strategy,* p. 230.

252. I. 143 (Jowett's translation).

253. Cf. Mahan, *Influence of Sea Power upon History,* p. 1.

254. Arrian, II. 17. 1.

255. *The Conduct of War,* p. 74; translated by J. T. Dickman, Kansas City, Mo., 1896.

256. Plut., *Anton.,* 64.

257. Polyb., I. 20.

258. I. 59.

259. *Epistulae,* X. 8. 4.

260. Silburn, *op. cit.*, p. 58.

261. *Ibid.*, p. 139.

262. Since the Carthaginians retreated under orders, with the intention of permitting the Roman dispositions to be scattered by the confusion of pursuit, it is more accurate to speak of the Roman formation as *designed to break the line*. In the *diekplous*, 'sailing through,' ships penetrated the enemy's line, but did not necessarily break it.

263. *Anton.*, 66.

264. Veg., IV. 44.

265. I. 49.

266. Torr, *Ancient Ships*, p. 92.

267. *Alexander*, p. 5.

268. Plut., *Moralia*, 331.

269. Thuc., I. 124.

270. IV. 31.

271. *Op. cit.*, pp. 139–140.

BIBLIOGRAPHY

I. MILITARY

ANONYMOUS, "Caesar's Art of War and of Writing," in *The Atlantic Monthly*, XLIV. 273–288 (1879).

BAUER, ADOLF, *Die griechischen Kriegsalterthümer*, in Iwan von Müller: *Handbuch der kl. Altertumswissenschaft*, IV. 1². 3. Munich, 1893.

BOUCHER, COLONEL ARTHUR, *L'Anabase de Xénophon (avec un Commentaire Historique et Militaire)*. Paris, 1913.

CREASY, E. S., *Fifteen Decisive Battles of the World*. New York, 1851.

DANIELS, EMIL, *Das antike Kriegswesen*. Leipzig, 1920².

DELBRÜCK, H., *Die Strategie des Perikles, erläutert durch die Strategie Friedrichs des Grossen*. Berlin, 1890.

DENISON, COLONEL GEORGE T., *A History of Cavalry from the Earliest Times*. New York, 1913.

DODGE, BREVET LIEUTENANT COLONEL T. A., (a) *Alexander*, (b) *Hannibal*, (c) *Caesar*, in the *Great Captains* series. Boston.

DROYSEN, J. G., *Heerwesen und Kriegführung der Griechen* (Hermann, *Lehrbuch der gr. Antiquitäten*, II. 2). Freiburg, 1889.

DU PICQ, COLONEL ARDANT, *Battle Studies, Ancient and Modern Battle* (translated by Greeley and Cotton). New York, 1921.

GIBBON, EDWARD, *The Decline and Fall of the Roman Empire* (Bury's edition). London, 1909–1914. See chapter 1 especially.

GILBERT, G. E. L., *The Evolution of Battle Tactics*. London, 1907.

BIBLIOGRAPHY

GROTE, GEORGE, *A History of Greece.* London, 1851–1856.

GRUNDY, G. B., *The Great Persian War and its Pre-liminaries.* London, 1901.

GRUNDY, G. B., *Thucydides and the History of his Age.* London, 1911.

HOGARTH, D. G., *Philip and Alexander of Macedon.* New York, 1897.

HOLMES, T. RICE, *Caesar's Conquest of Gaul.* Oxford, 1911^2.

JOMINI, BARON DE, *The Art of War* (translated by G. H. Mendell and W. P. Craighill). Philadelphia, 1879.

JUDSON, H. P., *Caesar's Army.* Boston, 1888.

KROMAYER, J., *Schlachten–Atlas zur antiken Kriegsge-schichte.* 120 maps and text. Leipzig, 1922.

KROMAYER, J., *Antike Schlachtfelder in Griechenland.* 3 vols. Berlin, 1903–12; vol. 3, Italien u. Afrika.

LLOYD, E. M., *A Review of the History of Infantry.* London, 1908.

MOMMSEN, T., *A History of Rome* (translated by W. P. Dickson). New York, 1900.

NAYLOR, WM. K., *Principles of Strategy.* Fort Leaven-worth, Kansas, 1921.

OMAN, C. W. C., *A History of the Art of War: the Middle Ages.* London, 1898. (See chapters 1 and 2.)

Pamphlet on the Evolution of the Art of Fortification, Number 58, Occasional Papers, Engineer School United States Army, Prepared under the Personal Direction of Major-General William M. Black, Chief of Engineers.

PAYNE–GALLWEY, SIR RALPH, *A Summary of the History, Construction and Effects in Warfare of the Projectile-Throwing Engines of the Ancients.* London, 1907.

ROBINSON, C. E., *The Days of Alkibiades.* New York, 1916. See Chapter VI, *A Land Battle,* for a picture of battle emotions and tactics.

BIBLIOGRAPHY

II. NAVAL

CUSTANCE, ADMIRAL SIR REGINALD, *War at Sea, Modern Theory and Ancient Practice*. London, 1919.

CLARK, F. W., *The Influence of Sea-Power on the History of the Roman Republic*. Menasha, Wisconsin, 1915.

FISKE, REAR ADMIRAL BRADLEY A., *The Art of Fighting: its evolution and progress with illustrations from campaigns of great commanders*. New York, 1920.

HALE, J. R., *Famous Sea Fights from Salamis to Tsu-Shima*. Boston, 1918.

MAHAN, CAPTAIN A. T., *Naval Strategy*. Boston, 1911.

MAHAN, CAPTAIN A. T., *The Influence of Sea Power upon History, 1660–1783*. Boston, 1898. See especially pages 13–21.

RAWSON, E. K., *Twenty Famous Naval Battles, Salamis to Santiago*. New York, 1899.

SILBURN, P. A. B., *The Evolution of Sea-Power*. London, 1912.

TORR, CECIL, *Ancient Ships*. Cambridge, England, 1895.

Our Debt to Greece and Rome

AUTHORS AND TITLES

AUTHORS AND TITLES

AUTHORS AND TITLES

AESCHYLUS AND SOPHOCLES. *J. T. Sheppard.*

GREEK RELIGION. *Walter Woodburn Hyde.*

SURVIVALS OF ROMAN RELIGION. *Gordon J. Laing.*

MYTHOLOGY. *Jane Ellen Harrison.*

ANCIENT BELIEFS IN THE IMMORTALITY OF THE SOUL. *Clifford H. Moore.*

STAGE ANTIQUITIES. *James Turney Allen.*

PLAUTUS AND TERENCE. *Gilbert Norwood.*

ROMAN POLITICS. *Frank Frost Abbott.*

PSYCHOLOGY, ANCIENT AND MODERN. *G. S. Brett.*

ANCIENT AND MODERN ROME. *Rodolfo Lanciani.*

WARFARE BY LAND AND SEA. *Eugene S. Mc-Cartney.*

THE GREEK FATHERS. *James Marshall Campbell.*

GREEK BIOLOGY AND MEDICINE. *Henry Osborn Taylor.*

MATHEMATICS. *David Eugene Smith.*

LOVE OF NATURE AMONG THE GREEKS AND ROMANS. *H. R. Fairclough.*

ANCIENT WRITING AND ITS INFLUENCE. *B. L. Ullman.*

GREEK ART. *Arthur Fairbanks.*

ARCHITECTURE. *Alfred M. Brooks.*

ENGINEERING. *Alexander P. Gest.*

MODERN TRAITS IN OLD GREEK LIFE. *Charles Burton Gulick.*

ROMAN PRIVATE LIFE. *Walton Brooks McDaniel.*

GREEK AND ROMAN FOLKLORE. *William Reginald Halliday.*

ANCIENT EDUCATION. *J. F. Dobson.*